How to Be an Ethnographer

To Professor Zofia Sokolewicz, one of the founding mothers of contemporary Polish ethnographic tradition, who firmly believed that ethnography is something you do with and for Others. We were incredibly lucky to have known her and practiced ethnography with her.

How to Be an Ethnographer

Monika Kostera

Professor Ordinaria, Faculty of Sociology, University of Warsaw, Poland and Södertörn University, Sweden

Paweł Krzyworzeka

Associate Professor, Management in Networked and Digital Societies (MINDS) Department, Kozminski University, Poland

Edward Elgar
PUBLISHING

Cheltenham, UK • Northampton, MA, USA

Published by
Edward Elgar Publishing Limited
The Lypiatts
15 Lansdown Road
Cheltenham
Glos GL50 2JA
UK

Edward Elgar Publishing, Inc.
William Pratt House
9 Dewey Court
Northampton
Massachusetts 01060
USA

Paperback edition 2024

A catalogue record for this book
is available from the British Library

Library of Congress Control Number: 2023935292

This book is available electronically in the **Elgar**online
Sociology, Social Policy and Education subject collection
http://dx.doi.org/10.4337/9781800883949

ISBN 978 1 80088 393 2 (cased)
ISBN 978 1 80088 394 9 (eBook)
ISBN 978 1 0353 4297 6 (paperback)

Printed and bound by CPI Group (UK) Ltd, Croydon, CR0 4YY

Contents

Boxes

Introduction to *How to Be an Ethnographer*

Nancy Harding and Monika Kostera (2021) introduce their book dedicated to contemporary ethnographic methodology, with an emphasis on practice:

> The derivation of the word 'ethnography' is from the Greek 'ethnos', meaning 'a people' and 'graphy', meaning writing, so ethnography literally refers to writing about people. This omits ethnography's most important aspect: it is an active, agentive practice – the ethnographer 'goes into the field', spends a more or less extended time living in and studying a community, and returns to their desk to write up their experiences, deriving meaning and insights as they do so. But, curiously, there is no verb 'to ethnograph'. (Harding and Kostera 2021: 1)

This practical aspect was the firm conviction and lifelong dedication of Polish ethnographer Zofia Sokolewicz, to whom this book is dedicated. Zofia wrote and published prolifically, mainly in Polish and in German, but she considered authorship to be just one among many ethnographic activities and not the central one. She believed in practices and in the building of structures and relationships, in education, in conversations, in making people meet. We, the authors of his book, met thanks to her ethnographic match-making activities. She had a vision of people building ethnographic communities and making them flourish. Whichever structures she had access to she used for that purpose. Departmentalization of knowledge was something that she strongly opposed. In every institution Zofia Sokolewicz developed, she made sure that everyone has access to both the knowledge and the structures and that diverse voices were present, regardless of their disciplinary background.

She would have appreciated the title of our book, we feel. She would have approved of our ambition: to introduce, in as simple words as possible, the impulses and ideas that can be used to *do* ethnography, understood as a way of engaging in social study, of approaching learning and other people, of growing as a human being and social creature, of relating to each other. Our own disciplinary backgrounds influence the selection of ideas as well as examples, indeed, of the topics themselves. However, the book is also intended as an open and welcoming invitation to ethnography. It is not another methodology book; there are many of these and we refer to some in this book. It is not an ordinary handbook for students and novice researchers, although it can certainly be used as such. Neither is it an ethnography in the usual sense: a narration of the findings of a research project concerning a community of people, even though it contains many short accounts of such projects. So what is it, if not these more obvious kinds of book?

The closest to a more fitting category for our book would be that of a DIY-manual-but-with-other-people, or Do-It-Yoursel(ves), if such a term existed. Ethnography is impossible to do by oneself, and we do not just mean the subject of ethnographic study, which is other people, but the entire sense of the engagement. In each chapter we both explain and encourage the Readers to test the various methods. We have included some examples of how others, including experienced researchers, as well as novices and absolute beginners, have used the methods for their research projects. We also discuss issues that are not directly about the tools and techniques, but, rather, moral and methodological principles as well as community related modes that are important and helpful for doing ethnography. Even if one uses all the techniques and methods correctly but lacks the *spirit* of doing ethnography, there still may not come anything particularly worthwhile out of it. In addition, what is *ethical research* differs for ethnographers from STEM-inspired researchers and, possibly, is even more important to be concerned about. While this little book is far from exhaustive in any way, we hope it will encourage and inspire our readers to grab further works, some of which we recommend. The bibliography can be used as a reading map, and more texts can be found in each of the listed bibliographic positions.

BOX I.1 DISCOVERING THE MUSEUM OF MY OWN CITY (GRADUATE PROJECT), BY MAŁGORZATA GRAMATNIKOWSKA

During my last semester at the university, I took a course on the creation of art – an activity understood not as a momentous act requiring special preparation, inspiration, practice and talent, but as the fulfilment of a very human need that lies dormant in every human being and can be carried out by him or her in many different ways. As part of the final work, we were required to conduct a short ethnographic research project and to present its results to other students. I decided to do a study of the Museum of Warsaw, which happens to be the city where I have lived all my life. I visited the Museum of Warsaw four times on Thursday mornings to see how museum visitors and employees interacted with the exhibited objects, as well as with each other, and with me. For the first time in my life I made an attempt at an ethnographic research project. Also, I visited this particular museum for the first time. When I first saw it as a researcher, I did not know how to behave, whom and for how long to observe, which observations and events should be considered important or at all noteworthy. However, I soon started to perceive something that intrigued me. I realized that the visitors' interactions with the museum have their own rhythm and dynamics. I noticed a certain repetition of events – emerging patterns. But simultaneously I also noticed the single moments, their uniqueness, and deviations from the patterns.

Visitors followed arrows painted on the floor. The tour began in the office in the basement. The visitors then made their way up the stairs to go through the remaining exhibition halls and view the items on display. The objects collected by the Museum of Warsaw were exhibited in such a way as to allow visitors to look at them, without showing immediately ready-made descriptions or interpretations. For this purpose, the descriptions (and often also the signatures) of the items were hidden in pull-out drawers, so that the visitors could decide for themselves whether they would like to explore the context of the object they are looking at. Over time, I noticed that some of the guests, when casting their first look at an item, didn't look for a description at all. I thought of the items as elements of many personal stories, directing the observers towards memories. I had a similar feeling when one of the guides, who was leading a group of people from Ukraine, displayed a certain item used every day in the kitchen. She did not explain it but wanted to draw attention to the common experiences of Poles and Ukrainians. Both groups were able to recognize the tool indicated by the guide, which in her opinion distinguished them from the guests from Western Europe. But there were also other visitors and employees of the museum who explicitly shared their knowledge and suggested how to explore the written history of the artefacts.

During my lonely visits to the museum, I did not stay alone but met several other guests. Some advised me to use the audio guide or catalogue to find out more about the items on display. I was also accosted by the exhibition supervisor, who showed me her favourite artefact and told me much more about it than I could learn from the information attached to it. And it is this human aspect of the whole experience that I value most in ethnographic research. When I entered the field, even one so dominated by *objects,* I learned to see *people* and saw them quite differently during my research. I saw how, surrounded by objects that have a significant impact on them, they were social actors in a context. This also made me think about myself. A visit to a museum, ethnographic research of the everyday history of my own city, made me realize the need to constantly learn about myself, about ourselves – a need that arises from human nature.

The example in Box I.1 presents a presentation held by one of Monika's students. She received emails from other students after the presentations praising this project. Several persons believed that it was particularly illuminating for them, an eye opener regarding the need for ethnography. They spoke of the human dimension that Małgorzata emphasizes. But not only that. One of the students who came from another city and did not particularly like Warsaw, said that this project made her look at Warsaw with more sympathy. She decided to try to like it. She also said that thanks to this project she now intended to visit the museum of her own city. She ended her email with the reflection that

> [g]oing to a museum by yourself does not have to mean loneliness. People talk about things and things remember people.

So welcome. Please try it at home. Invite your friends and enjoy. Like nature, ethnographic research works on the principle of abundance – the more of it, the more diverse it gets, and the more energy is generated.

1. Entering the field

1.1 A SHORT HISTORY OF THE ETHNOGRAPHIC FIELD

Researchers conduct ethnography in all fields imaginable, including both distant cultures and lands, and our most mundane workplaces and organizations. And yet, some historical and contemporary ethnographic traditions hold a relatively narrow vision of a legitimate ethnographic research field. In this chapter, we start with the presentation of those more orthodox ethnographies and views of what constitutes the ethnographic fields. Learning about the origins of ethnographic research begins with the field and is crucial for understanding the specificity of ethnography in general. And so, we will take our readers on a trip to Siberia, the Polish countryside, Australia, Tikopia Island, and US towns to finally arrive at business organizations in industrialized countries and virtual communities. This journey will show how important it is to consider different notions of how to define the field. It is a question of research design – but also an important theoretical decision. Moreover, when a researcher takes for granted what constitutes a legitimate research field and does not devote much attention to this aspect of research, they do not escape these questions but they remain hidden: there are some implicit ontological assumptions. Such hidden assumptions may weaken the entire research project. Ethnography relies strongly on reflexivity and conscious focus (Goodall 2000). The vignette in Box 1.1 shows how a well-known and quite mundane place becomes an ethnographic field thanks to such a focus on the part of the ethnographer.

BOX 1.1   SAME OLD GROCERY SHOP, EXCITING NEW FIELD (GRADUATE PROJECT), BY LAURA MISZKOWSKA

Examining the grocery shop, I expected the obvious: the energy, the crowds, the organized work, the annoyed people queuing to the counter, perhaps a prevailing confusion. And thinking about the employees, I sensed that I would see fatigue and work in constant motion. Going into the field proved to me that what I expected was but a narrow part of their world. The world we all seem to know, the world we live in every day. During a pilot study I already realized how little we see when our role is just to be a customer. It's as if we don't want to see many things then, and we interpret situations in a quite superficial way. When the aim is just to do the shopping, all the senses are not in focus, they are, is if, relaxed.

A local shop is not only about queues and wandering customers asking for the best product or the location of particular products. It is also a space of neighbourly conversations, words exchanged by shoppers: compliments, enquiries about private life, people chatting about the weather. While walking between the aisles one can hear various conversations, not only those related to the area itself, but gossip and news from mouth to mouth both between customers and from customers to employees. The shop assistant is not just a salesperson. For regular customers he or she is also a listener, a conversation partner and even a neighbour. This is a neighbourhood, after all. The bonds between regular customers and neighbourhood shop employees are quite visible. Even if I would expect such observations in a small neighbourhood shop, the atmosphere really surprised me.

But looking from the perspective of the duties and responsibilities, a shop assistant is also not just a salesperson, either. It's a job that requires quite wide skills. It is important to organize and communicate, to know the goods, the codes, basic product knowledge: to be able to recommend something, to build up trust. It is important to have a good knowledge of sales to be able to place orders. Shop assistants try to keep the customer satisfied, the shop properly stocked, and the owners not suffering losses. This job also requires physical strength: setting up the shop, moving goods takes strong legs and spine. It is mainly a standing job. The duties of a shop assistant show that he or she is, yes, a salesperson, but also designer, cleaner, and on top of all that, an emotional labourer with a smile on their face.

A shop is hardly an exotic place. It is part of everyone's everyday life, common and connected with everyday duties. A researcher's sensitivity makes it possible to see the less obvious aspects of 'shop life'. It is by studying this mundane field that I realized that ethnography really *is* an adventure and a journey. Even when it is not very exotic, it is still interesting. It doesn't matter what kind of field we explore, the inspiring thing is that the deeper we go, the more fascinating and creative the process becomes, observations allow us to have new ideas and ask new questions. Even in this initially rather uninteresting place. After conducting this pilot study, I left the site with more doubts and question marks in my mind than I thought possible.

Some anthropology departments organize the diversity of fields hierarchically. They rarely do this in a formal manner, but in practice they often do: the valuation of fields is visible in academic practices such as hiring, financing research, and general prestige. In addition, some locations seem to be more ethnographic than others. As Gupta and Ferguson write, based on their US experience, it is not unusual to regard 'Africa more than Europe, southern Europe more than northern Europe, villages more than cities [...] according to the degree of Otherness from an archetypal anthropological "home"' (Gupta and Ferguson 1997: 13). In other communities, such a hierarchy of fields also exists.

While working on my PhD, I, Paweł got a job at the State Ethnographic Museum in Poland. My departmental colleagues were seasoned ethnographers and nationwide experts in folk costumes, farm tools, and traditional crafts. Joining the museum, while finishing my doctorate at the university anthropology department, exposed me, then a young ethnographer, to two ethnographic traditions. First, ethnography is frequently misunderstood by those of us studying folk culture. In many European countries, ethnographic museums focus on describing and preserving folk culture, the culture of peasants and the countryside in general. Second, there also exists a widespread tradition to regard ethnography as a research approach to studying contemporary social phenomena. In the case of my research project it was a cultural aspect of emotions in a multi-level selling organization. Yet my colleagues in the museum did not recognize the PhD project as a legitimate ethnography. For them, the field should be quite specific and this, by itself, clearly defined 'ethnography'. And so, ethnography was, to them *the countryside* and an interest in 'traditional culture', which is usually divided into three categories: material culture (e.g. tools, architecture), spiritual culture (e.g. religious rituals, art), and social culture (e.g. kinship relations, social norms). Researching business organizations was, to them, a misuse of the term.

The possibility of studying ethnographically contemporary phenomena, for example, business organizations, results from a more than century-long evolving process. Nevertheless, one can still meet ethnographers who adhere to the literal meaning of ethnography according to which it stands for *writing ethnos*. The Greek *ethnos* means: folk, people, and nation. For these orthodox researchers, the employees and managers of mundane workplaces are not part of the *ethnos*.

But even if one takes to heart this traditional, literal meaning of ethnography as describing the *ethnos*, even here we can see a variety of traditions. After the collapse of the USSR, regions in the post-soviet territories became an intensively studied research field. Researchers outside of Russia got access to areas that were previously quite restricted. The restrictions applied not only to Western scholars but also to ethnographers from socialist countries in central Europe such as Poland. I, Paweł, joined the new wave of studies, and my ethnographic skills were forged by studying Belarus and then Siberia. The unique opportunities emerged from observing evolving cultural, national, political, religious and economic processes of an opening country with an enormous diversity of languages, religion, culture, ethnic histories, and complex relations between groups. Academic ethnographers did not discover that field only in 1990s. There existed studies published previously by Western ethnographers, such as an excellent monograph on a Karl Marx Collective Farm in Buryatia by Caroline Humphrey (1983). However, the peoples of Siberia have been almost exclusively covered in many highly detailed and specialized publications by generations of domestic Soviet ethnographers. Doing and writing ethnography in Buryatia, the UK social anthropologist was engaged in different academic activities from soviet ethnographers, which helped to add perspective on the studied field.

In the early days of ethnography, after the First World War, the *ethnos* school predominantly focused on small-scale, isolated groups. Studied groups inhabited Indian reservations or islands such as Tikopia, of Trobriand Islands, studied by famous ethnographers Firth and Malinowski. The field, back then, was defined by easily distinguishable boundaries of a single society and could be characterized by three main features. First, the organization of these groups relied on personal relationships. The small scale allowed researchers to study the whole group. Second, the field was substantially different from the researchers' society. Third, those groups typically lacked written texts. These three characteristics of the initial field sites are no longer predominant in the academic community of ethnographers but they may help to understand some of the key further developments in ethnography.

Claude Lévi-Strauss points out that studying societies which researchers were drastically unfamiliar with forced ethnographers to abandon their beliefs, prejudices and methods of thinking (Lévi-Strauss 1975: 2). As a result, they could grasp aspects of social life that enriched our understanding of humankind in general. To achieve that unique understanding, they had to go beyond the existing methods of studying societies, as history, literature studies, law and philosophy heavily relied on analysis of written documents, which in fields such as Tikopia were absent. As a result, not only has observational research been developed, but ethnographers started applying a holistic approach, gathering material in various ways and forms. Besides developing new research techniques, early academic ethnographers formed a specific vision of culture as an integrated system based on consensus and shared characteristics. This vision is still shaping popular understanding of culture. In some cases, even academics find it instrumental in their analyses, even if they no longer study encapsulated distinct and relatively coherent social groups.

The vision of an encapsulated culture, which was formed back in the times of the origins of ethnography, became a potent metaphor – and it is oftentimes still in use. On the one hand, the concept is helpful as it offers a sense of having a manageable unit of analysis:

> bounded, coherent, cohesive, and self-standing: social organisms, semiotical crystals, microworlds. Culture was what peoples had and held in common, Greeks or Navajos, Maoris or Puerto Ricans, each its own. (Geertz 2000: 248–249)

On the other hand, the concept of discriminate cultures obscures the complexity of social organization, and blurs the evolving boundaries, frictions, and conflicting values. The early idea of an enclosed culture was handy for academic purposes and political processes because, for those in power, a helpful fallacy is embedded in the concept of culture. While any group's culture and social organization are dynamic and incoherent, the early conceptualization of culture only identifies culture with the dominant discourse. It was silencing weaker voices. We can also find this narrow vision of culture in management studies, where organizational culture, in many cases, is just a control tool used by those in power (Deal and Kennedy 2000 [1982]). Ethnography is not about such narrowing down of focus. Studying organizations ethnographically, researchers should open up their cultural vocabulary (Martin 2002).

After researching small isolated groups, anthropologists moved their engagement first to bigger and more mixed-up objects such as India, Japan and Brazil. This move happened after the Second World War. The original concept of culture as shared feelings and values could not be maintained when faced with the observed dispersion. As Geertz put it:

> What makes Serbs Serbs, Sinhalese Sinhalese, or French Canadians French Canadians, or anybody anybody, is that they and the rest of the world have come, for the moment and to a degree, for certain purposes and in certain contexts, to view them as contrastive to what is around them. (Geertz 2000: 249)

Anthropologists followed the path trailed by Geertz of abandoning reified discrete space-bound objects of studies, even when still doing observational research in one location. Instead, it has been pointed out that collective life 'takes place on a dozen different levels, on a dozen different scales, and in a dozen different realms at once' (Geertz 2000: 254), not limited to one studied location.

Currently, many types of field are considered legitimate, including 'ethnic' and more mundane studies. At the beginning of the twentieth century, the approach to studying social groups developed by Bronisław Malinowski became a recognizable research method. As a result, some researchers saw an opportunity to use his study method in other settings, such as industrial communities and their own societies. This 'ethnography at home' was born during Elton Mayo's study in the Hawthorne Works factory near Chicago. The research project was long and complex. The results, however, were inconclusive. Researchers found it hard to make sense of, for example, how diverse variables that researchers were manipulating (e.g. lighting, work time, breaks, providing food) influenced shop floor workers' productivity. Finally, the study became iconic and founded the influential Human Relations Movement. One can even say we would not have HRM as we have now if not for that project.

Lloyd Warner was an anthropologist who worked under Bronisław Malinowski's supervision and conducted his research in a traditional ethnographic field, a native Australian tribe. He had the grand idea of applying what he had learned in Australia to study his American society. Elton Mayo invited Warner, believing he could contribute to the study by using his developed observational methods – skilled in fieldwork. Not only did his ethnographic skills impress Mayo, but also his unusual experience in the distant field. In Mayo's words, his colleagues were interested to hear of Warner's 'wild experiences' with 'Australian savages' (Gillespie 1993: 155).

Warner, the ethnographer in the factory, did not feel he was in the right field. First, it was very limiting for him to operate within the factory walls. His anthropological experience made him approach a studied phenomenon as an element of a broader social system. Workers' productivity, Warner hypothesized, could have been a result of the disintegration of a social system outside the factory. Many of the workers had moved to the town recently, leaving their home towns and countries, family members and friends. They had withdrawn from the social organization that gave them safety. In the small town, which at that time was an Al Capone headquarters, they faced a lack of the social organization they needed for safety and wellbeing. The emerging social organization in the workplace, making friends and forming cliques to support each other, influenced the work. However, this interpretation did not make it into official findings. Lloyd Warner left Hawthorne to start his project in New England, where he could study the whole social organization, including organizations such as societies and factories, but not as separate entities, research fields encircled by factory walls or lists of members. However, he was limited to one town and treated it as a village.

Nowadays it is popular to focus on a single organization and not to treat it as a 'village'. It is known as organizational ethnography. When applied in organizational studies, ethnography faces problems similar to the historical definition of culture and the object of study. Scholars and practitioners who perceive ethnography just as a research tool are tempted to study organizations as if they were tribes or villages. The version of organizational ethnography we are describing here is different. For many years, organizational ethnographers did not recognize their active role in constructing the field. The fact that organization, as a field, was something given and recognizable was an obstacle in the development of organizational ethnography. The full potential of ethnography as a holistic approach, not limited to reified boundaries, was not developing fully.

Even some early organizational ethnographers perceived their role as those who see through the factory walls (Baba 2009), not limiting their field to the boundaries of formal organization. However, recent theoretical developments in organization studies lead us to focus on organizing beyond organizations. And this creates an even more favourable climate for ethnography. As a result, ethnographers changed the way they conceptualize the field. Nowadays, we focus on processes: on organizing instead of an organization. This terminological shift results from two processes. The first is a debate about the ontological nature of organizations. There are adherents of both the school of viewing organizations and processes and as solid states. The distinction is not quite crucial for ethnographers, as they can study both. The second is more relevant to them: the changes in the nature of capitalism, emerging new forms of labour and organizing open calls for a new, dynamic approach. Ethnography can now develop its full potential as reified clear boundaries of formal organizations no longer constrain it. But it is the third, methodological, reason that is the most valid: ethnography cannot lead to general theories or laws and it cannot speak for the entire population. However, it can very well represent social processes longitudinally, i.e. as something that develops and gets repeated in patterns – culture.

It was postmodernism that initially destabilized conventional organizational analysis. Postmodern academics privileged a weak ontology emphasizing what is emergent and ephemeral (Chia 1995) instead of organizational grand narrative. Questioning the ontological foundation of societies and organizations, social scientists challenged the previously predominant practice of focusing on the individual organization as an object of study. Instead, they claimed we should study 'the production of organization rather than organization of production' (Cooper and Burrell 1988: 106). In this way, researchers started to focus on practices that constitute what is *perceived* as social settings and organizations. Abandoning the organization as an analytical category, caused some destabilization within the discipline but certainly helped to appreciate the focus on social processes. As Sverre Spoelstra (2005: 113) puts it, 'being occupied with organizations is thus a way to stop thinking about organization'. Organizations started to be regarded as not being 'social facts' but 'ongoing accomplishments' (Cooren et al. 2011). Nowadays we have a choice, we can focus on process or on facts. But the way we study this phenomenon should reflect that theoretical development. A contemporary ethnographer can – but does not need to – study community organizations as if they were villages or islands, looking for their unique characteristics. She can – but does not have to – uniquely pay attention to what people do, what is happening, what patterns develop.

Some important socio-economic transformations fuelled this shift towards complexity in thinking about social settings. Human life in many parts of the world used to be a series of transitions from one to another closed environment 'each having its own laws: first, the family, then the school ("you are no longer in your family"); then the barracks ("you are no longer at school"); then the factory; from time to time the hospital' (Deleuze 1992: 3). Information technologies allowed for the emergence of more open societies than those of disciplinary societies that reached their limit in capital accumulation. The new society, called the 'society of control', offers unique opportunities for extracting value within freedom under control. It is a complex society but unaware of its own complexity. In those contemporary societies, people are 'free' to do whatever they want, but their behaviour is influenced by new, indirect forms of power. In parallel to the development of the new type of society emerged new forms of organizing and labour, which are also more open, ephemeral and often invisible as they take an immaterial form. In this context, it is not only interesting but truly enlightening and potentially liberating to be able to show how this complexity is organized and how it develops. It is easier and also safer to alter processes than to shift states and eradicate facts.

Communities and social settings are nowadays also changed due to the increased exposure to social media platforms and IT. For example, billions of users perform free immaterial work by posting and interacting digitally on major social media platforms (Beverungen et al. 2015). However, companies owning those platforms formally employ only a tiny part of the total number of people engaged in labour. This change of modes of capitalist production influenced organization theory that included these production processes in its analysis. Because the production of value escapes the walls of the corporation and enters everyday life through 'immaterial labor' (Mumby 2016) this leads ethnographers sometimes to include consumers in the research fields we construct, as it is almost impossible to separate consumption from production, as consumption becomes the act of co-production.

The American cultural anthropologist George Marcus observed that the problems which ethnographers study are rarely located conveniently in one place. Marcus calls for abandoning the practice of single-location fieldwork: he suggests that we follow individuals, metaphors, stories, conflicts, ideas and things. His argument derives from the economist Robert Solow's thought that

> there is not some glorious theoretical synthesis of capitalism that you can write down in a book and follow. You have to grope your way. (Marcus 1995: 98)

That 'groping' for ethnographers means doing, what he calls, 'multi-sited ethnography', a research strategy designed around conjunctions, paths, and chains, not inside a single location. This practice is inspired by constructivism as introduced by the early twentieth century avant-garde. At the outset of a project, the phenomenon, an organization, is only loosely defined and tentatively outlined. The result of such constructivist-like ethnography is a map of a cultural phenomenon, which also contains patterns – patterns are important in most contemporary ethnographies, whatever the espoused ontology.

But not everything is 'just fluid'. Claude Lévi-Strauss (1975) observed that the field is changing, either because of changes in native cultures that became more similar to the researchers' culture, or because anthropologists may have moved their interest to their societies. He concluded that research methods should change as well. However, his prediction has not materialized. On the contrary, it turned out that the research approach shaped in the unique circumstances of a small-scale, illiterate and unfamiliar research field offers a valuable and refreshing quality even when applied to studying contemporary industrialized societies.

Choosing a research field has not only methodological and theoretical consequences but also some pragmatic aspects. Mayo presented Warner as an attractive persona who studied 'Australian savages'. Our research fields influence the reception of researchers and their findings, for better or worse. The anthropological hierarchy of fields does not apply universally to other disciplines. However, in other disciplinary contexts, the valuation exists but can be different. For example, the ranking of research fields in management is a reverse version of the anthropological one. Anthropology's highly valued field sites usually have minimal economic power, making them less attractive to mainstream management. Organizational and workplace researchers who gain international reach, work in countries with high GDP or economic growth. Doing ethnography at home does not diminish the attractiveness of their research. As a result, few organizational ethnographies draw on organization studies and management in Africa – which is a serious omission, which, we hope, will be remedied in the near future.

1.2   THE ETHNOGRAPHIC COMMUNITY

The field also defines the academic community which we, ethnographers, interact with. The most typical intellectual community embraces ethnographers from the same or similar fields. Even if their theoretical and research topics are different, they see the value in meeting and interacting. Someone doing research in Siberia, Africa, the Mediterranean, the Pacific or Australia, will probably know and follow other ethnographers working in those regions. This trend is less visible in workplace and organizational ethnography. This shows that it is, indeed, not geography that unites researchers. It is experiences. Doing ethnography in organizational settings has integrative power as it exposes researchers to similar experiences and methodological challenges.

For example, ethnographers studying spirituality and religion in Amazonia have several possible communities to debate. Some are doing the same in the region, others are working in Amazonia, and others are studying religion in different areas. Even when researchers share neither research field nor research interest, they still can enrich each other as they all practice ethnography. It is not uncommon for ethnographers to read ethnographic monographs outside their direct interest just because they are good ethnographies. Motivated by a general interest in culture and social relations, one can find analogies and inspirations from even distant fields that can inform our research (Figure 1.1).

	The same research field	Different research field
The same research interest		
Different research interest		

Figure 1.1   The intensity of intellectual interactions between ethnographers: darker shade means greater intensity

Choosing a field means joining a specific academic community. This may influence the choice of the field. We may want to become members of a particular group because of their proximity or intellectual attractiveness. As the field has a defining power, career choices are also uncommon, especially in circumstances where a clear hierarchy of domains is visible. Specialization in different fields gives different career options.

Not all fields are attractive and 'nice'. Some are plainly dangerous. One can see a significant discrepancy in the measured level of safety even within the OECD countries. OECD Better Life Index (OECD 2020) takes into account metrics such as homicide rate and subjective 'feeling safe walking at night' to state that Norway is the safest country (9.9) and Mexico the least secure (0.2) in the OECD countries. However, ethnographers often chose even more dangerous countries than those least safe in OECD, such as active warzones. Safety considerations should also be considered in countries from the top of the safety rankings. For example, studying drug dealers and street violence in Norway (Sandberg 2008) poses ethnographers more hazards than researching elite schools in South Africa (Kenway and Koh 2013), i.e. the top and bottom countries from the OECD safety index, respectively. The rankings focus mainly on interpersonal violence. We can, however, distinguish other types of danger that can arise during fieldwork. The nature of activities we would need to engage in to participate can lead to accidents. Ethnographers study workplaces with a high degree of occupational hazards, for instance, fishing boats, construction sites, factories, warehouses, and climbing routes in the Himalayas. Danger can also be derived from natural disasters, harsh climates or epidemiologic situations. Moreover, the limited availability of reliable healthcare may contribute to the severity of the abovementioned dangers.

Challenges may come in other forms than directly threatening our physical health and life. For example, fields could require a researcher's high emotional labour. Moreover, meeting ethnographically with injustice, poverty, homelessness, illness, and even death may not be for everyone. So we need to ask ourselves, when choosing a field that may expose us to human suffering, whether we have the capabilities to tackle this burden.

Very often, ethnographers choose a field because of the existence of cultural distance. Still, this distance can also be a source of problems that may undermine the project and personal wellbeing. For example, ethnographers can experience discrimination based on age, gender, ethnicity, religion, social status, and political views. If we can expect a high probability of severe adverse reactions, we should assess whether we are able and willing to deal with the consequences.

Preparing to conduct ethnography in distant, unknown or high-risk field sites, novices can learn from more experienced ethnographers by reading their monographs and methodological essays. In ethnography, methodological literature is often devoted to the intricacies of being in the field and not to the correctness of practical material-gathering techniques (Lee 1994). After learning about potential hazards, one can develop safety procedures in cooperation with their university, such as an emergency evacuation plan in case one needs to leave the site quickly. Possibilities of access to medical help should also be explored. It is not true that good health insurance always solves the problem. In some regions, using informal institutions may be more effective. And, finally, one should consider arranging psychological support, including the aid of a professional psychologist.

Bronisław Malinowski's fieldwork on Trobriand Island offers a prime example of an ethnographer's psychological challenges. He experienced loneliness and monotony of life far away from home. He was afraid of diseases and felt frustration and anger with the natives. We learned about Malinowski's struggles from his intimate diary published posthumously (Malinowski 1967). Writing the journal was a coping mechanism for Malinowski, and writing such diaries is still prevalent in the field. Nowadays, we ethnographers use our felt emotions and bodily experiences as a source of knowing the field, and there is a place for those records in published ethnographies (Van Maanen 1988).

It is not just the other academics that form the ethnographic community; so does, of course, the field and its regular inhabitants. In ethnography, the field is truly foundational; as a result, it is the field that often initiates the project. This marks out ethnographic engagement as different even as far as qualitative social studies go. Generally, the research problem is the proper starting point in social research. After that, other elements such as data gathering methods and data sources should achieve the main aim. However, the nature of the research problem and research questions in ethnography explains its field-first approach. Ethnographers approach the field open to surprises, with loosely defined research questions. They know that pre-existing assumptions about the problems may change and probably should change if the research is well-executed. As initially defined by researchers, the problem is less critical than real problems emerging from the field. But this is only one methodological explanation of the centrality of the area in ethnography. Others are pragmatic and identity-based.

Finally, the ethnographer's private social context is also, in a way, part of the ethnographic community. Personal and family considerations may play a role when choosing a field. Traditional anthropological fieldwork can last a year or longer, which means moving to the area for a year and staying there can have consequences for family members. In addition, the partner's job, children's school, friends and family, and safety need to be considered. Among anthropologists doing fieldwork far from home, we can find many spouses involved in the same field, e.g. Edith and Victor Turner, Hildred and Clifford Geertz, and Jean and John Comaroff.

BOX 1.2   ON THE BENEFITS OF BEING A MEMBER OF THE ETHNOGRAPHIC COMMUNITY, BY ANNA GAŁĄZKA

When we say that 'the whole is greater than the sum of its parts', a phrase attributed to Aristotle, we allude to the power of a collective, an organization, or a community that is greater than ourselves. Feeling part of a greater whole helps us flourish. As a relational sociologist shaped by the writings of Pierpaolo Donati and Margaret Archer (2015) on our relational nature 'through and through', I strongly believe that our social life is embedded in our relations with one another, and that we must form positive and enduring connections with what matters to us. Ethnography as a practice for knowing about the world around us matters to me, and ethnographic communities represent the said communal 'whole'. Ethnographic communities have only begun to be studied systematically very recently (Bieler et al., 2021); they can have many names and take many forms. What unites them is their focus on ethnographic practice – thinking about, doing, discussing, sharing, supporting, critiquing – the list goes on.

There are great emotional and social benefits of being part of an ethnographic community. As is the case with many academic groups, engaging with like-minded scholars can alleviate the stress and loneliness associated with a lone presence in the foreign land we study and create a sense of accountability for making our internal musings captured in the fieldnotes visible for constructive critique (Hastings et al. 2022). This is important because ethnography is full of tensions. It is at the same time rigorous and improvisational. With its origins in the anthropology of Malinowski, it has, over the years, evolved to include an array of ethnographic field engagements, including 'quick and dirty' medical ethnographies (Vindrola-Padros and Vindrola-Padros, 2018), such as the one I completed for my doctorate into clinician–patient relations in wound healing. Without formal training in anthropology, ethnographers from a multitude of backgrounds can easily feel anxious about what they do and what they discover (Yanow 2009); therefore, being part of a community where these feelings can be safely articulated can help us deal with what Yanow (2009) calls 'methodological performance anxiety and nervousness' and give us greater confidence in our work.

On an epistemic level, community collaboration across disciplinary divides offers further gains. Communities are a rigorous yet friendly platform for the deconstruction of the often confusing and overwhelming data we collected on our own. As observed by Bieler et al. (2021), our individual ability to reflect on our practice may quickly reach its limits when considered within the bounds of individual mental capacity; community collaboration can strengthen our interpretative authority through a continual scientific review of knowledge production. This can spur (collaborations on) publications for getting our ethnographic voices heard.

Indeed, my ethnographic community has grown over the years around the Annual Ethnography Symposium – an interdisciplinary meeting of ethnographers around the world, which allows those interested in ethnographic practice, regardless of their disciplinary background or the extent of training, to form networks, share ideas, get feedback, and gain social and emotional support. This vignette – one I am extremely flattered to have been invited to provide – is a product of a serendipitous encounter during an annual meeting of my ever-growing ethnographic community. I encourage you, Dear Reader, to keep cultivating yours.

1.3   ACCESS

The final choice of the field results from many forces, sometimes conflicting, such as when an ethnographer, based in a university or business school, has unique access to an intellectually intriguing organization in Malawi. But at the same time, her senior colleagues warn her that Malawi is not an important enough place. Supporting this argument, they share first-hand experiences of how journal editors rejected their articles about Polish family firms because 'nobody cares about Poland', as a reviewer wrote. But the researcher may take other aspects into consideration, not only issues related to rational incentives that benefit their career. Ultimately, curiosity and serendipity may tip the balance toward one field over another.

Once chosen, the field, whether it is an organization, a village, or an online community, will guide the research both as to design and empirical findings. The ethnographer leaves her home to find answers to her research questions – and to find new questions, not thought of before. When faced with reality, other, more precise, more important formulation of research problems may emerge. As Evans-Pritchard wrote about his ethnography in Africa:

> I had no interest in witchcraft when I went to Zandeland, but the Azande had; so I had to let myself by guided by them. I had no particular interest in cows when I went to Nuerland, but the Nuer had, so willy-nilly I had to become cattleminded too. (Evans-Pritchard 1976 [1937]: 242)

When ethnographers approach the field they follow ideas. The preliminary ramifications are no more than a scaffolding which fades away as the followed problem becomes central and initial. But the importance of the field does not disappear. Sites may be multiple but are still sites. Like Douglas Holmes (2000), following the idea of nationalism in European politics led him to Italian villages and the European parliament. The ethnographer has to decide on a starting point: organization, village, neighbourhood. Methodological, practical, and identity considerations still apply.

An ethnographer usually does not seamlessly transfer from choosing a field to being in the field. There is an essential phase of getting access, when we negotiate if we will be allowed to get in. During the fieldwork, we define the access's ramifications with the gatekeepers. This process influences how we will be perceived or defined by the study group members but is also a source of information about the studied groups. We start our field work before we gain access to the field.

Some fields are hard or near impossible to study because of their closed character or sensitive nature. In the latter case, researchers often decide not to interfere. On the other hand, there are fields where we can determine that the intensive presence of the researcher could have negative consequences, for which the potential benefits from the study outcomes do not compensate. In such cases, we may limit our research to conducting interviews or using other, less intrusive research methods. Sometimes, however, access could be a factor positively influencing field choice. Maybe there is a unique opportunity to gain access to a particular field. It may be a community or a workplace organization where the researcher has already gained trust which, for an outsider, it would not be possible to get.

In more conventional ethnography of distant societies, getting access had its spatial aspect. 'Getting there' required organization of transportation. The trip could take several days or longer. However, the journey already marks an opportunity to start doing an ethnography. It may be worthwhile to talk to the people one is encountering, to experience nature and the travel itself. For ethnography at home or organizational ethnography, the transportation aspect could easily be missed as getting to an office in a skyscraper in the city centre is not as engaging and problematic as getting to a remote village on another continent. However, as commuting is a daily practice of organization members, ethnographers can include this activity in their observations and fieldnotes.

Getting there means also being accepted by the group as a researcher. The initial contact with the field is limited to a single person or a small number of group members who will introduce the researcher and let him in. Who those people are may actually influence how the ethnographer will be perceived and treated by others. In the case of organizational ethnography, there may be no choice but to start with managers, as their formal acceptance may be required. However, this may create a barrier when contacting employees. They may perceive the ethnographer as a management person. These initial contacts with powerful actors helps, in some cases, to build trust. But in many others it creates barriers which may be difficult to eradicate.

Formal organizations are a popular way to get initial contact with any other field. For instance, Juan José Martínez d'Aubuisson (2019) studying MS-13 gang in El Salvador, contacted a charitable, church-based organization. Ethnographers are representatives of academic organizations. This allows making semiformal contact with local institutions. The formal function and communication channels (e-mail address, phone numbers) allow for relatively easy initial contact.

It is worth remembering that knowledge sharing cannot be conscripted. That is why gaining access is not about one single moment. Even if formally, after signing an NDA, the researcher is allowed to talk to organization members and participate in their daily life, it is not an ethnography yet. Each research participant will decide how much they would allow them to enter their life, and ethnographic research is all about building of relationships. Getting access is a longer process because gaining trust takes time. One can even regard fieldwork as an ongoing getting access exercise, when we build rapport and learn the culture, including language or professional lingo, to be allowed closer to the local perspective.

Language is an important consideration as well as part of the accessibility (if not always directly 'access') to a field. Ethnographers try to use the local language or at least learn it on the way while doing their research. Language is crucial for understanding the group under study. Later, when writing up ethnographies, they need to refer to the specific aspects of the language to build a meaningful representation of the other. That is why there are so many monographs terms written in the native language, and not necessarily in 'global English' – despite the current pressures on academics to publish in English. When choosing a field, it is important to assess available means to learn the language and our abilities and willingness to acquire a new language. Language is not an important consideration when choosing a field for those doing ethnography at home. However, even if the researcher speaks the local language, he may not be fluent in a specific (for that field) vernacular. It is imperative to also be open to learning a professional subculture's dialect. The dialect is essential to understand the culture and determine the level of access to the field.

BOX 1.3   GETTING OUT INTO THE FIELD, BY KATARZYNA KRÓL

I conducted my ethnographic fieldwork in the Samegrelo region of Georgia at the tea factory. Back then, I was in my mid-twenties, which definitely worked both to my advantage and disadvantage on various occasions.

In my experience, getting access to the field was a process and it was far from linear. Rather, it was an ongoing negotiation to access new layers of the field while not losing the ones already established.

I was lucky enough to identify my potential gatekeeper in the initial phase of my research, still in Tbilisi, who through a mutual acquaintance agreed to meet me at the time of her visit but, in the end, could not make it. I used it as an excuse to visit her in her hometown a few days later with the intention of convincing her to participate in my endeavours. The idea of a foreign girl arriving at the gate of the tea factory seemed to be bizarre enough to convince her to let me observe her work. Also, my age and gender, and the fact that I was alone and far from home played a crucial role in her positive decision to take care of me.

But for several months I could not access the tea plucking team – it was very clear that they were not interested to talk to me or work with me. Partially due to the fact how labour-intensive tea plucking is, partially to the relationship I had with my gatekeeper – as she was responsible for assessing the quality of the tea leaves they brought each time, communication between the pluckers team leader and my gatekeeper remained tense. I also made a mistake. When I was finally invited to join pluckers in the tea field and work with them, I forgot where my solidarity should be. After several months with my gatekeeper, I knew that I should only collect the best, the most delicate top leaves of each tea bush. But that was the strategy only I could afford – as pluckers are paid per kilogram of collected leaves, they have to be more strategic in the amount and quality of collected leaves. I wanted to impress my gatekeeper so much with my skills that I focused on picking only the best ones. We came back to the factory so the leaves could be weighed and rated. My gatekeeper complained about the quality of the leaves brought by the team and praised me in front of everyone. How proud of myself I was. Until I saw the faces of the rest of the team. No need to say, it took me several more weeks to be able to go back to the tea field again.

This experience taught me that there is no such thing as a single event or person granting access to the field. And even though the factory seemed to me as one unit, within it, there were teams with varying interests. And I failed to identify with whom I should have aligned that particular day. Getting access to the field is not easy, but really challenging is not losing access once it is obtained.

Field access, if any, will be influenced by many factors. Over some factors we do not have influence. Our gender, age, race, and ethnicity may affect the access and the research process. In ethnography, the researchers are not transparent, invisible agents applying previously-designed research tools and techniques. Ethnographers are themselves an instrument of the inquiry. Who we are and what we do would influence the final results. Which is a delicate balance but it can work for good – nothing teaches us about humans as well as experience.

2. Who is the ethnographer?

2.1 ETHNOGRAPHIC ENGAGEMENT

BOX 2.1   THE ETHNOGRAPHER WHO BECAME AN
ORTHODOX NUN IN MACEDONIA, BY
PAWEŁ KRZYWORZEKA

The undergraduate ethnography programme I studied exposed me to field-work experience very early. In my university, first-year students choose between a handful of thematic groups, so-called ethnographic laboratories. Up to the final third year of studies, supervised by more experienced researchers, ethnographic laboratory participants read the literature, plan their research project, participate in several fieldwork trips, and finally write their first short ethnography. I was interested in the post-soviet region, and I knew some Russian language already, so I picked the Belarusian laboratory. Our group was supposed to study ethnic relations and the national identity processes in Belarus. Most of my close friends, however, decided to join the Macedonian laboratory. A more demanding and exciting one. They were about to learn a new language and travel to the Balkan region to explore the religious practices of Macedonian Orthodox church members. This is a story about my friend Barbara who once went for fieldwork to Macedonia and never returned home.

Barbara was a shy and warm person. Fieldwork in Macedonia required her to hike in the beautiful mountains to get to remote villages, where she stayed with local communities to learn about their religious life. Barbara also visited orthodox monasteries located in early medieval stone buildings. In one of these places, she met a fascinating priest. He and a group of nuns spend time on prayers, everyday activities and making mosaics from colourful ceramic tiles. Each member of the ethnographic laboratory found a specific topic for their final project. Barbara was especially interested in monastery life. One of her Macedonian fieldwork trips became life-changing, as she decided to join the charismatic priest's group she studied. Not as a participant observer, but for good. She did not share her plans with anybody, neither with her parent nor with her closest friend who accompanied her on that journey. Barbara never finished her ethnographic studies, and she even didn't return to her family in Poland.

For the consecutive generations of ethnography students, Barbara's story became an example of going native. The term describes becoming a member of a studied community by internalizing their culture, values, and lifestyle. Twenty years later, students still hear about a young ethnographer who, as a consequence of researching ethnographically the Orthodox Christian church in Macedonia, became a nun. The story, in many versions, is shared even by those who never met Barbara. For this vignette, I contacted Barbara's friends from the Macedonian ethnographic laboratory to discuss possible lessons for our readers. Here is what we talked about.

We learned that while practising ethnography, we are more vulnerable than in our life outside fieldwork. While in the field, we try to understand the Other by switching into a highly receptive mode. We carefully listen, observe, and empathize. That increased level of openness and receptivity may create unique academic contributions but may also result, for the better or worse, in life-changing consequences for the researcher.

Another important point: interactions with research participants are two-way. We contact individuals to gather empirical material and answer research questions. They, however, like the charismatic priest from Macedonia, also may realize their agendas while hanging out with us. This fact can be easily missed when we are too focused on being an ethnographer. There is some background to the romanticized version of Barbara's story. The charismatic priest, during a short period of time, gathered a group of women from diverse European countries, who were all fascinated followers. The newly created community was not, however, recognized by the Macedonian church as a legitimate monastery. At some point, his group, together with Barbara, had to escape from the picturesque old building to be constantly on the run, living in rented flats in the capital city. From the data we gathered, the priest was actively recruiting foreign individuals who, by joining him, suddenly broke off all relations with family and friends back home, leaving close ones extremely anxious. The ethnographer is a liminal character but there are local actors, sometimes, who have their agendas concerning liminal characters.

We all hope that Barbara is safe and happy.

Sometimes it is said that, in ethnography, the researcher is a research tool. This analogy highlights the crucial role of the person doing the research. She is more important than the procedure or specific techniques. Indeed, ethnography engages individuals with their emotions, body, imaginations and often private

social relations. We will describe the challenges and opportunities created by
such a holistic method. The example in Box 2.1 shows that being a liminal
character, betwixt and between characters, contexts and life-worlds can be
complex and difficult as a position to hold. Hence, it is important to *know
oneself* in the field.

Ethnographers work in many different departments and have various edu-
cational backgrounds. Some ethnographers may not even work in academia;
they apply research findings in the industry. For us, the main groups of ethnographers that we refer to are socio-cultural anthropologists, sociologists,
and organizational studies and management scholars. We picked those groups
because of our experience of changing affiliations between those disciplines.
There are also influential ethnographies in education studies, healthcare,
nursing, gender studies and every other social science subdiscipline we know.

Ethnographers with different disciplinary affiliations have a lot in common,
hence they can all be called the same name as their fieldwork is similar. They
all share a body of critical literature they learn from. Some discrepancies
derive from the specificity of their disciplines. A crucial dimension is the
heterogeneity of their disciplinary community. Ethnographers in anthropology departments usually interact with other researchers regularly practising
ethnography. Their intended audience knows the methodology, accepts it or
even expects it. On the other hand we have the ethnographer in the accounting
department of a business school. Their colleagues, reviewers, and journal
editors have to be explained in detail what they do when they say they do ethnography. Ethnographers have to convince their community that this approach
is legitimate and valuable. In anthropology, ethnographers are the dominant
group. In accounting, they are an easy-to-miss minority.

Despite the methodological similarities, those diverse ethnographers are
excited about different research topics, analytical categories, and theoretical
inspirations. One may have five ethnographers from five disciplines studying
the same hospital, and they would produce five different ethnographic monographs. In ethnography, *who* conducts research matters more than in other
methodological traditions. Ethnographic research informs the reader of the
human perspective – which is never 'objective' but, rather, subjective and
inter-subjective. Despite the diversity, ethnographers share similar – different
from other research methods – experiences of engaging the whole self in
understanding the other. Hence, we need to discuss some aspects of the ethnographic self and what kind of challenges and opportunities we face by showing
up in the field.

We argue in the previous chapter that researchers actively co-construct
research fields. Multi-sited ethnography even makes this construction an
important goal of ethnography. In organization studies prone to taking the
field for granted and closing 'within factory walls', it is essential to highlight

the diversity of possible outcomes, which partially depend on who conducts the research. Let us use the Tamaraland metaphor developed by David Boje (1995).

The play *Tamara* by John Krizanc was one of the longest staged plays in Los Angeles. The play was based on a historical episode from painter Tamara Lempicka's life. What was specific about this play was that every spectator chooses their path through rooms where actors perform simultaneously. Depending on the viewer's choices, each audience member creates a unique version of the play, their own story that they leave the theatre with. We would like to encourage our readers to look at the field through the lens of this metaphor. Each member makes their own view of the community. The ethnographer is no different. The shape of the final ethnographic account depends on the researcher's decisions and other factors. In the play, each audience member came to see the same play but left with a unique story. Our experience of sociality or organizing is similar. We may be members of the same social setting, but our individual experiences are unmatched. A full spectrum of factors contributes to this remarkable result. Many of these factors are shaped but not entirely determined by who we are, by our aims, values, status, physical appearance, and social and cultural capital. This contributes to our actions, how others interact with us, and how we make sense of our experiences. An ethnographer similarly gets a unique take on an organization. As Gareth Morgan (1998) argued, it is impossible to grasp the whole organization in all its aspects, diversity and dynamism. Metaphors mediate our thinking about organizations, and each metaphor exposes some aspects of organizing while other aspects are hidden.

Annette Weiner arrived at Kiriwina, the largest of the Trobriand Islands, to study wood carvings that men produced in response to a new phenomenon of growing tourist demand. The phenomenon was absent 50 years earlier when Bronisław Malinowski did his ethnography in the same field. During Weiner's first day in the field, young girls took her to show a women-led funeral ceremony. For five hours, she observed local women who gathered in the centre of the village to exchange fibre skirts and bundles of strips of dried banana leaves. It later turned out that, in one day, women could distribute thousands of piles, worth several hundred dollars. This female-led specificity of the ceremony took Weiner by surprise as she had learned very little from Malinowski's ethnographic monographs about the role of women and their contribution to the local economy. As a result, Weiner decided to abandon her initial research topic and instead focus on the problem of exchange, already described in the literature topic. However, Weiner aimed to give an account of both men and women. As a result Weiner wrote a ground-breaking ethnography (Weiner 1976) that contributed to the development of theories on gift and exchange and became influential writing in feminist anthropology.

With ethnography, the importance of listening to the field prevails over sticking to the initial research problem. It was the field that 'told' Weiner what was the essential phenomenon, worthy of being studied. Her initial idea to explore wooden carvings made by men was an armchair idea only, which had to give priority to problems that emerged on the site when the ethnographer met the studied group. If she were not a woman, local girls would probably not have taken her to the ceremony in the first place. Her gender, life experience, theoretical orientation, preconceptions and assumptions, and personal values influenced the research questions, process and findings. So, indeed, the role of the researcher is the key in ethnography. And subjectivism is not a vice but a virtue. Or at least it is an inescapable feature of any ethnography.

Malinowski's and Weiner's exchange studies on the Trobriand Islands are different not only because of the gender of the researchers. They were also of different nationalities. Malinowski was Polish-British, and Weiner was American. However, they both had something significant in common. They were outsiders. In the 1970s, when Weiner published her monograph, the first generation of local anthropologists got their education at the University of Papua New Guinea. Research by local anthropologists started with criticism of foreign anthropologists' work and even its rejection. Papua New Guinean researchers criticized foreign colleagues for economic exploitation, stealing artefacts, 'failing to report back adequately and contribute to the community they studied' (Morauta et al. 1979). Their research differed considerably from those of overseas anthropologists. For example, Papua New Guinean researchers were more politically active. They did not separate research from social and political action, unlike the foreign researchers.

The term *native anthropologists* was initially coined to describe local researchers doing ethnography of their non-European societies or ethnic minorities in the United States. Later, the term was extended to ethnographers studying organizations to which they belong. Native ethnographers are perceived to have some advantages over outsiders. For instance, they are sensitive to the language used in the field. An outsider ethnographer can easily miss some nuances of a local language or occupational jargon. Additionally, native ethnographers have the advantage of trust. They have already got or can quickly gain trust. Moreover, by being a member, an ethnographer can uniquely describe and interpret local points of view as they co-create those interpretive frameworks (Jones 1970). But there are also some quite fundamental challenges of being a native ethnographer. The last thing a fish would ever notice would be water. Insiders can easily miss aspects of everyday life and not problematize them. An outsider researcher, in turn, may recognize elements that, for insiders, are mundane and boring details. Additionally, natives may also experience problems with distancing themselves from the field. As a member of the studied group, those researchers have unique emotional relations. They often depend on the group and may have long-time friends in the field. The processes that native researchers analyse impact their lives directly, not only in the research context, while an outsider participant-observer, even a very empathetic one, can distance themselves from the problem being analysed and interpret what they observe and experience.

The insider–outsider division is widely used. However, when we look at it closer, we see no one-to-one relationship between an insider ethnographer and the studied group. Some claim that the 'extent to which anyone is an authentic insider is questionable' (Narayan 1993: 671). There are many dimensions along which humans are aligned or set apart, and they are not all contained in a study. That vision assumes the older concepts of culture as something coherent that all members share. This vision is silencing the voices of those who do not identify with all the aspects of that particular culture. Culture, in this perspective, is a dominant discourse only, which pretends to be something else.

The insider researcher problem is twofold. First, the alleged insider may be only formally a member of this group, an employee, a country citizen, or a village inhabitant, but the group one is researching may be characterized by a high level of otherness for the researcher. Is a university professor studying her university administration or student life an insider? Is a Polish ethnographer studying farmers an insider if he was born and raised in the capital city and had never spent more than a few days in the countryside before? To some extent, they are insiders, but we can be misled by taking the insider/outsider division for granted. Instead, we should recognize the internal diversity of the field and the power relations there and only then reflect on the potential insider position of the ethnographer.

It is helpful to think about the insider status of a researcher as a situational characteristic. In some contexts, insider opportunities and threats are activated in the same field and with the same people. For example, a university professor may be an insider when talking with high decision-making university administrators, as they are engaged in the same processes. But this same professor can be an outsider when studying the topic of work hours, as groups have different experiences – administration working from nine to five, faculty with a more flexible schedule. Even when a professor becomes a student to do her ethnography, like Nathan (2006) did, she joins her field, a university, as an outsider.

Alexandra Jaffe studied the military. She describes how negotiations of meaning are strongly linked to the individual's organizational status. While conducting her research, she served as a US military officer. She describes her insider status not as a problem to be solved but rather an opportunity to involve her status in the understanding process. In her words: 'ethnography is not about resolving, but exploring the relationship between involvement and detachment that is part of life in general' (Jaffe 1995: 36). The experience of involvement and detachment during the fieldwork showed Jaffe that intimacy between insiders is built on implicit assumptions and shared knowledge, while intimacy between outsiders and people they study is built upon the apprenticeship process. That is why outsiders can ask questions that an insider ethnographer cannot, because it would destroy her legitimacy as an organizational member.

The appearance of a person is performative and it shapes her interactions with the research participants. It influences them to some degree. An ethnographer can, for example, decide to dress up for her fieldwork in an office environment or choose not to wear a formal suit. The body, however, is a real presence that is being brought to the fieldwork. Ethnographers occupy space and are identified based on their physical appearance as old, young, feminine or masculine, white, and friendly-looking. All this shapes the interaction. And similarly to insider–outsider status, we should not treat the researcher's body as a problem to solve but explore and learn from. Presence is one of an ethnographer's main duties and one of his best ways to gain experience in the field (Pachirat 2018). It serves as a source of knowledge. People use their bodies to participate in social life. Ethnography is one of the participatory social research methods grounded in bodily co-presence. Till Förster (2022), in his research among Senufo people in West Africa, developed a close friendship with Kartcha, a local research participant. This unique relationship had a secret interactional dimension that was unavailable to other people in the village. The friend was able to tell the ethnographer that she needed to meet with him later to talk about her problems with her husband or her husband's other wives or that she was planning to leave the village for the fields. Those acts of communication were ephemeral and subtle. For an observer, they were indistinguishable from everyday actions and random gestures. The ethnographer learned that other people in the village develop such relationships. However, it was impossible to observe them from the outside. If anybody from the outside could understand the subtle communication, it would not be this unique way of being together that is their own only. Förster identified its existence because he developed such a close relationship with a friend from the village. When he described this phenomenon, he referred to the Jasperian concept of *leibhafte Bewusstheiten*, the 'feelings of bodily presence'. He said he and Kartcha developed 'increased sensory awareness to the subtleties of bodily presence in social life' (Förster 2022: 5). During interactions with Kartcha, this participatory, bodily experience was clear and distinct. However, the challenge was to capture this non-observational knowledge in words. Förster, in his fieldnotes, used metaphors that best-approximated the experience he and Kartcha shared but he still felt a lot was lost in this translation. The researcher's body gives access not only to hidden social practices, as in the African example, but, sometimes, building upon our bodily experiences provides access to the locals' ways of thinking. The body becomes a medium to access their world of perception.

The ethnographer depends, unlike positivist researchers, on intense and personal engagement. But what happens when she studies other intensively engaged people? Studying activism is challenging because of its high intensity, weakening activists' bodies and even causing injuries. Participant observation of activism led ethnographers (Rahmouni Elidrissi and Courpasson 2021) to experience that aspect of activism. Rahmouni Elidrissi was engaging in activism as a participant observer and was surprised that she pushed her own body to it limits due to intensive work, physical and mental exhaustion, and sleep deprivation. She 'forgot' her body, sacrificing it for a more significant and urgent cause. As the experience was challenging, she recognized it as an opportunity to develop reflexivity and gain non-observational knowledge. Personal experience of physical breakdown allowed the ethnographer to realize the centrality of the body in activism and how people respond to organizational control.

Bodily experiences as a source of knowledge are more accessible to newcomers. When a new physical experience surprises an ethnographer, they can identify and reflect on it. After some time, however, the habituation process makes the experience more normal and less pressing to problematize. Förster, in his African ethnography, acknowledges that the new and surprising experience became part of his everyday life after some time. Outsider ethnographers are better positioned to read their bodies and use them as a source of knowledge. When we engage in certain practices during a prolonged period of time, we develop routines and no longer focus on them consciously (Förster 2022).

2.2 STUDYING 'UP' AND 'DOWN' SOCIAL HIERARCHIES

Ethnographers may study 'up' or study 'down', as their relations with the field are asymmetrical. Social class, economic status, personal wealth, and cultural capital define the unequal levels of research interactions. Conventionally, ethnography was often about studying down: colonizers studying colonies, educated studying illiterate, richer studying the poorer. Nowadays, however, this unidirectional power imbalance in the field looks much more complex. Ethnography is no longer in the service of colonizers and the powerful and, indeed, very often ethnographers see themselves as working for the benefit of the powerless and underprivileged (Goodall 2000). Ethnographers are also frequently studying up; for example, they are researching elites. There are also situations where it is not clear who is 'higher' or 'lower'. Or, as in the following example, the ethnographer's initial assumption about the social hierarchy can be changed and even overturned due to research.

Amanda Krzyworzeka (2013) conducted her ethnography in Poland, which is her native country. For her fieldwork, she moved from the capital city to a small village in one of the poorest regions in Poland. Polish ethnographers have traditionally studied peasant culture and the countryside. The first ethnographic descriptions of the peasant culture were made in the context of a feudal society by those higher on the status ladder, the nobility. Even during the socialist decades, studying the folk culture was dominated by the identification of a number of inequalities. This local, post-colonial heritage made Amanda Krzyworzeka, who was born and raised in the capital city, weary of potential distortions deriving from her position of relative privilege. She approached her study with caution and sensitivity to status and power relations. However, those relations turned out to be, in many cases, asymmetrical, but in the opposite direction than for her ethnographic predecessors. Contemporary Polish farmers living in this region nowadays run high cashflow agricultural businesses, own spacious houses, and have more than one car. The region is indeed less privileged but this holds true for urban inhabitants, not for the countryside. Most of the farmers themselves, or, if not, then their children, held college degrees. For them, the ethnographer living on her PhD scholarship, which was not higher than the official minimum wage, was someone considerably lower placed in the social hierarchy than themselves. Farmers often expressed their pride in their superior economic status. However, the ethnographer is not someone devoid of power. When Amanda Krzyworzeka left the field, she acquired a symbolic power status. The ethnographer exercises power and takes responsibility for creating a representation of the culture. As the topic of Krzyworzeka's research was the economic practices of the farmers, her research informed directly or indirectly how those in power, such as policymakers and journalists, perceive farmers' economic actions. Studying farmers turned out to be studying up only during the fieldwork.

Sometimes ethnographers knowingly approach fields positioned as a higher status group. Doing it consciously does not make it unproblematic. Studying elites makes it even harder to access the field than in other areas. Studying up may bring an ethnographer into an uncomfortable position, not just in connection to feelings of inferiority but due to his relative deficiency of means to accompany and take part in the life of the studied field. How do you do participant observation of managers whose standard lunch costs more or less your weekly lunch budget? However, here also, the asymmetry of power and status relations that we assume, may change once we learn about the group ethnographically. By understanding the group, it is possible one may discover that the privileged are just as entangled in social hierarchies as the less privileged. Sometimes they may turn out to be powerless victims of the complicated power relation in that field. For example, those studying Hollywood actors and actresses realized that, in the Hollywood constellation of producers, directors and others, actors and actresses are not as powerful as it might seem from the outside. Similarly, despite their wealth and public attention, top-earning athletes are involved in complex social relations that limit their agency and power. Those studying top management, another classic example of studying up, learn from the fieldwork that elite and powerful individuals are often bound by organizational inertia and bureaucracy, as well as – especially in recent decades – in relations of anonymous ownership and algorithmic dependencies, which deprives them not just of power but of job satisfaction, as a group of Monika's students realized a few years ago. 'This was one depressing study!' they concluded during the presentation of the results, 'and yet we thought we would be studying something out of an idyllic lifestyle magazine'.

BOX 2.2   WE HELP THEM FINISH THEIR STUDIES
           AND WRITE THEIR PhDs, BY MAGDALENA
           BODZAN

I conducted research among people with refugee and migration experience. I was interested in solidarity initiatives that were oriented around cooking. I conducted participant observation at cooking workshops and interviewed both the people who organized the events and the refugee women themselves.

It seemed to me that power relations were clearly defined here. Those with migration and refugee backgrounds were supposed to be the ones I was studying down. Because of their experience of violence in their country of origin, as well as of arrival, where they experienced dehumanizing procedures, limited access to housing, job market and discrimination. All of this turned out to be true, but only partially. Studying up or studying down is a concept that changed relationally.

First, it turned out that the community itself was composed of not equal individuals. One of my interviewees, when she learnt who else participated in my research, said: 'Oh, so you have not only refugee gastrocelebrities?' By gastrocelebrities, she meant people who had come to Poland some time ago, learnt the language, and had higher education and permanent jobs, often in NGOs. They made 'being a refugee' their side job, in which they performed an image of a 'good refugee', which was important for the initiatives that aimed not only at supporting people in need but also at convincing Warsaw residents that 'refugees are people just like us'. Some start-up initiatives were even starting their ventures with such contacts, as 'well-known refugees' looked better in city grant applications.

Second, the privileged position of white Europeans, including researchers, from the perspective of research participants is problematic but not in a way researchers may assume. For the people with refugee experience I interviewed, more problematic was not that researchers enjoyed more privileges than the group studied but that they tried to rhetorically mitigate that inequality or even reverse it.

I want to share a final thought expressed by one of the women of refugee background with everyone who is planning to study refugee and migrant communities:

> If they want to face the guilt, they could start by appreciating that a woman who made her way from a faraway country without a visa, without money, without acquaintances, and was able to make her way into it, is a valuable person to the movement. Such a person cannot be treated like a child who is learning life. We are trying to explain to our allies that we are not victims and that we do not need help. We need people to work with us. Sometimes girls from the university come to us and ask, 'how can we help you?' We end up being the ones who help them... finish their studies or write their PhDs. We are a living material for them.

2.3   ETHNOGRAPHIC KNOWLEDGE

The realization that the result of ethnographic research relies heavily on who conducts the study was recognized even by early ethnographers. Evans-Pritchard explicitly formulated the following thought 'what one brings out of a field-study largely depends on what one brings to it' (Evans-Pritchard 1976 [1937]: 241). Claude Lévi-Strauss (1975) even argues that ethnographers are learning mainly about themselves and their culture by studying other cultures. Ethnographic knowledge is created in an interaction between the researcher, the field and the audience. In Chapter 1, we discussed the role of the field. In this chapter, we reflect on the centrality of ethnographers in the research process. This means not only the role and the presence of the ethnographer as a person but also the development of knowledge that is taking place during the study. The whole point of ethnographic research is that being in the field is transformative for the researcher. Ethnographers change their initial approach to the field. Our preconceptions and even research problems deeply grounded in theories and previous research findings will change. It even happens sometimes that the ethnographer, after the research, becomes something of an antithesis of the person he was when starting the project. One should keep this in mind when engaging in such research. It does not leave the person neutral, untouched or virginally detached. This process of transformation is connected to deep learning and it resembles a hermeneutic circle, where meaning emerges from particular circumstances.

BOX 2.3   ETHNOGRAPHIC REFLEXIVITY, BY
          MAGDALENA LUBAŃSKA

The ethnographic method is a type of qualitative research that distinguishes itself from other social sciences by stronger/intensified reflection, i.e. a constant reflection on the status of one's own cognition and its entanglement in a specific socio-cultural-environmental context. While conducting research, we constantly think about how the way in which we perceive the world and what we know about it influences what we see and understand in the field. But we also try to determine what we can do to make it a feedback loop process and how to achieve it. We need to question our knowledge under the influence of what we have learned from the people we met. For ethnography is, like Gadamer's hermeneutics, the art of understanding and interpretation. I agree with Gadamer that in order to understand something, one must treat one's initial knowledge as 'forethought' and revise it, allow The Other to question it. Hans Georg Gadamer (2006 [1960]), whose cognitive approach is very close to ethnographic sensitivity, recognizes as the ideal moment of meeting The Other a situation where we experience a so-called 'merger of horizons'. This is the moment when each side of the dialogue begins to notice a new cognitive horizon, somewhere between, or above one's own arguments and those of the other party. For me, it is identical to the moment when I spot an important interpretative lead and when I feel that I have finally understood something crucial for my research.

In the Bulgarian Rhodope Mountains it was, for example, a situation where a Muslim woman who was about 30 years old (the daughter of a hodja, that is, a teacher of Islam), and asked about the reason for performing wudu (ritual purification), explained to me that it was a consequence of the consumption by Adam of the forbidden fruit. Describing the ritual impurity that happened after the consumption of the forbidden fruit, and the desire to correct this situation, she did not use knowledge from the Koran. But, as I later discovered, her story contained many threads analogous to those described in the tenth century by Al-Tabari in *Quisas Al-Anbiya* (*Lives of the Prophets*). It was an important lead in the research because it showed me that in the Rhodope Mountains, in addition to Islam inspired by Salafi theology which is used to educate hodjas studying, for example, in Saudi Arabia, you can still come across post-Osman Islam and the religious teachings popularized in that branch of the religion.

I remember when a young local farmer, in an interview I had with him, described stories told by the woman as local folklore, completely unaware that her stories can be inscribed in a wider socio-cultural context. By trusting the knowledge of the interlocutor, ignored by the hodja, I was able to

describe the various currents of Islam in the Rhodope Mountains more ac-
curately and adequately. I found that the 'Lives of the Prophets' played
a role analogous to the apocrypha in Christianity, and that in the Ottoman
Empire they were repeated and considered part of the religious tradition.
The Islam professed, inter alia, by the said female interlocutor was one
I could conceptualize as adat Islam (from the Turkish word 'adat', custom,
as local customs were accepted by the Hanafi Islamic school practised in the
Ottoman Empire). After years of ethnographic practice and experiencing of
many analogous situations, I believe that field research is an excellent way
to reach cultural messages that do not fit into the recognized canons of culture created by the dominating group. A passion for pluralism and a desire
to know and describe the perspective characteristic of what is 'borderline'
in relation to the ideological options dominating in society, as well as a humility towards your own initial cognitive assumptions – this is what, in my
view, defines ethnography.

As we can appreciate from the example, humility is important for ethnographers. Indeed, it does matter who it is that conducts ethnography, and this goes
far beyond researchers' skills and experience. Ethnographers use the whole
self, their identity, their body and mind to gain an understanding of the other.
As a result, it is hard, if not impossible, to separate the empirical material from
the researcher. Those who conduct ethnography analyse the material, interpret
it and write up findings. Even teams doing ethnographic research do not split
into subgroups gathering material and interpreting and analysing data. This
would be pointless and sterile. One can say that the format of ethnographic
material is usually messy. Frequently only the authors can navigate it. Trying
to codify and clean it up would result in a loss of valuable insight. The complicated and 'chaotic' form of field notes results from methodological holism
– gathering material requires an ability to deal with very complex material.

Moreover, ethnographers' knowledge is broader than any notes are able
to capture. As Polanyi famously said, 'we can know more than we can tell'
(Polanyi 2009: 4), and we can add that we can tell more than we can write
down. Interacting with fieldnotes, with the literature and theories, ethnographers also use not recorded knowledge, called headnotes. In the next chapter,
we describe the research process, what 'being there' looks like and why it
results in a particular, idiosyncratic format of the empirical data. This requires
a high degree of awareness and reflexivity (Goodall 2000).

Even a very experienced ethnographer such as Frederick Barth (Hylland
Eriksen, 2015) may encounter problems working with someone else's fieldnotes. He once took the task of finishing a project that his colleague had not
completed because of his death. Barth went to see the field to make sense of

a deceased colleague's fieldnotes. Familiarity with the land's spatial configuration, distances, places' contours, and heights was essential for understanding the fieldnotes. These aspects were omitted in the fieldnotes. However, if the original author analysed the notes, those headnotes would interplay with what was recorded (Hymes 1996). Both the authors of this book keep such notebooks with us, and they sometimes look like extremely complicated scripts, alternating between text, doodles, images, models, keywords and fragments, like sketches of complicated architectural structures. Needless to say, these notebooks are deeply personal and we rarely show them to others – and if we do, only to other researchers.

The ethnographer is a central character in the narrative – even if humility is much required. Consequently, contemporary ethnography purposefully uses first-person accounts so as not to leave the reader with a false impression that the research process could be detached from the researcher. We present the ways of writing ethnographic research in a separate chapter.

3. Looking and being

3.1 OBSERVATION

The British art critic, novelist, painter and poet John Berger wrote in one of his much loved books, *About Looking* (1991 [1980]), about a way of looking that connects the observer and the observed through the net of meaning we all are immersed in, as inhabitants and co-creators of culture. Everything we, humans, see is located within the realm of a culture. Without it, we would not be able to exist as human beings. Another great author, interested in culture, albeit from the standpoint of anthropology, Clifford Geertz (1973), believes that the human 'is an animal suspended in webs of significance he himself has spun' and 'take[s] culture to be those webs, and the analysis of it to be therefore not an experimental science in search of law but an interpretive one in search of meaning' (p. 5).

Berger's book is a guided journey through these nets. He proposes that human vision can be used to see intensely: beyond surfaces and into the deeper levels of meaning. Seeing overtakes definitions, explanations, even names themselves.

Seeing comes before words. The child looks and recognizes before it can speak. But there is also another sense in which seeing comes before words. It is seeing which establishes our place in the surrounding world; we explain that world with words, but words can never undo the fact that we are surrounded by that world. The relation between what we see and what we know is never settled. Each evening we see the sun set. We know that the earth is turning away from it. Yet the knowledge, the explanation, never quite fits the sight (Berger 1991, p. 7).

By looking this way, we can learn to understand what we see. Otherwise, the study of culture would be as hopeless an endeavour as the striving of a fish to experience the water. As the water is for the fish, so is culture for the meaning-spinning human being. Whatever we experience we take in and interpret as meaningful – or else, we do not experience it at all. Meaningless things are chaos to the human mind, they fall outside of what it is able to absorb. Berger proposes that looking can be used to see in-between the meaningful and the meaningless, that the gaze can be purposefully directed at the yet unnamed and held like this, in order to catch meaning as it is born.

One of the most classic ethnographic methods, observation, is based on the same principle, if not limited to the sense of sight. As we shall see in the next section, it can be based on intense looking, just as Berger proposed. But the original and most popular methods of observation involve all the senses. Indeed, as Timothy Pachirat so succinctly reminds us in his beautiful dramatization of ethnography, *Among Wolves* (2018), ethnography is very much a method of research based on the authority of *being there*. Studying something ethnographically means establishing a direct, mutual and deep bond with the studied reality, based on physical presence. The ethnographer does not work through intermediaries, she does not send out pollsters working for her, she does not explore the world as mediated by numbers. In the words of organizational ethnographer Dvora Yanow, who wrote the foreword to Pachirat's book, it is 'the most human of methods' (2018: xii). By means of her presence in the field, and experiential attentiveness to it, the ethnographer discovers and expresses what it means to be human and how we are and can be human together.

BOX 3.1   'HE ACTUALLY LEFT HERE WITH THREE JACKETS', OR ON OBSERVING SECOND-HAND SHOPS, BY WIKTORIA GLEŃ, AGATA MOLENDA AND IZABELA RZĄD

Kraków, AD 2021. A room looking like something out of an old-fashioned interior decoration catalogue: sterile white walls and winding conversations among rectangular furniture. What is this: a movie plan, a nostalgic café? No, this is a second-hand clothing shop in Kraków. The hangers are full of vintage clothes, a selection of which decorates the shop windows. Another shop packed with colours and shapes of the 1990s, characteristic typefaces and movie posters adorning the walls. Some plants and original antiques, as well as photos of old stars and loud, pop music. In addition to this décor there are also popular films, books and TV series, as well as some gadgets. Yet one more shop: several customers searching for second-hand clothes in huge bins and long rows of hangers, the only spots of colour against the white walls and floors. We observed all these strange, slightly eerie and sometimes rather magical interiors for many days, all in all five different small shops located in different areas of the city. At first we did not participate, but were more or less hanging around and taking in the general atmosphere. In particular, we were focusing on the interactions between people. Then we were taking part in the interactions between people in three of the shops we studied. Thanks to the kindness of the employees in these places, the researchers became regular 'guests' of the organizations and were able to conduct longer research, focusing also on the interactions that shoppers and shop assistants had with them. We chatted informally and also conducted some formal interviews with both customers and shop assistants. We also engaged with the merchandise, and had some interesting conversations with people visiting all these places about their preferences, tastes and motivations when choosing second-hand clothes. The people we saw visiting these shops, and chatted with, were of different ages but predominately female. Indeed, everyone we talked to was female.

By being there we realized that these shops are much more than places for shopping. The first impression was not incorrect – it was perhaps something of an imaginary movie plan or make-believe community café. They were meeting places for the local community. We also found that the space of the shops was as important as the interactions taking place in them. The shop's approach to clothing selection, the interior design, the smell of the interior, the arrangement of the clothes and decorations, the price and the salesperson's attitude to the customer – all these things defined the identity of the place as much (or more) than the merchandise itself. While observing these shops we had a strong feeling that each of them should be treated individually, on its own terms. It is then they become really interesting.

The aim of ethnography is not to see the general, the main, but to perceive the individual, 'on its own terms', as the authors of Box 3.1 say. The classical ethnographic methods are directly anchored in this mission. In particular, there are two such methods: non-participant and participant observation (for a wider presentation, see Kostera 2021). Non-participant observation means that the researcher tries to take in the studied situation from the outside, without taking part in any of the social roles existing within a culture.

Michel de Certeau (1988 [1974]) used non-participant observation to explore urban space. Walking through New York City, he admires the surroundings from the point of view of a pedestrian, a railway passenger, a passer-by. Even though a big city dweller himself, he carefully preserves the point of view of a stranger: a sense of wonder and awe that helps him to see a bigger picture and the context of what he observes. He comes to realize the role of space in human culture, how it is experienced, what role it plays in other experiences, what it helps us to see and to do. The everyday reality of the city, observed by de Certeau, such as coffee and sandwiches served on the train, the views moving along outside, form not just images – which he beautifully depicts in his small stories – but a big mental architectural drawing of culture. On the basis of these experiences, de Certeau delineates strategies – the rules created and guarded by the structures of power – and he puts forward tactics

– ideas that can be used by people moving around the social and structural spaces which are defined and made possible by these strategies. To de Certeau, the urban space is composed of planned strategies, as well as of the tactics of the inhabitants, adopted for everyday use: the shortcuts, trespasses, squats. The inhabitants create their own living city within the official one, a city constantly under construction. Both strategies and tactics can be mapped by observation, which, ultimately, helps to create a more or less complete and comprehensive map of cultural reality.

The second great classical ethnographic method is participant observation, where the researcher enters a social setting and becomes a participant in order to understand it and explore its culture. The American sociologist William Foote Whyte (1993 [1943]) studied a deprived immigrant (Italian) urban community from within. In his book *Street Corner Society* (1993), he calls it Cornerville and presents as a rich and complex setting of interwoven social roles, set against a larger context of a difficult time and the bigger US society of that era. What interests him most of all are the formal and informal ways of organizing and community building. Renting a room from a local family and learning Italian, he is truly a participant ethnographer, taking part in the day-to-day routines, sharing the problems, and some of the informal activities of the community. Thanks to the trust he has been granted by the community, he is allowed to participate in its more authentic ways of life. He learns to empathize, to understand. He develops a wish to help the people he has been studying, to make a real difference in their life – not just leave to write an academic thesis. After having finished his field study, he remained engaged in the problems of the studied community, often together with one of his research participants, known in the book as Doc. He was profoundly convinced that the ethnographer needs to understand the studied field and act and speak for it so that its conditions may improve. This kind of deep empathy can be only born out of shared experience.

Both classical types of observation have their advantages and disadvantages, and in many regards they complement each other. Non-participant observation is often strikingly insightful, but at the cost of detachment and disconnection from the real problems of the field. Participant observation comes with the risk of losing distance and 'going native' – the researcher gains engagement but loses the broader perspective needed to be able to collect interesting and multifaceted field material. Of course, both types can be applied in the same field, even if not at the same time. There also exist hybrid methods such as direct observation and shadowing.

Direct observation is a combined method: in part non-participant – the researcher does not become an insider – and, in part, participant – the researcher follows the customs in the field. The ethnographer is able to keep her distance but does not have to extract herself completely from the studied context. Whenever she does not understand something, she can ask a research participant to explain. But she is able to remain in her role as researcher and does not have to take part in all the activities of the studied community following the same rules as the insiders. She can come and go in her own rhythm and as it suits her other schedules and duties. Perhaps the latter provides one of the important reasons why so many students of organizations tend choose this method – nowadays many researchers do not have the possibility to completely engage in research and have many other duties. This makes the study at risk of being less engaged, but, on the other hand, it gives the researcher a unique possibility to look at the studied field from the point of view of many different hierarchical and subcultural perspectives. An interesting example of how this method has been used is Gideon Kunda's *Engineering Culture* (1992). The researcher observed middle-level management in a modern American corporation for six months (the whole project took one year and included, in addition, interviews and text analysis). He wanted to understand how the corporation strived to 'manage its culture' and what influence this had on everyday life and work of the employees. He also wanted to know how people reacted to these attempts and dealt with them. The methods he employed enabled him to see the corporate everyday life from two perspectives: the top management's and the middle managers'. As it turned out, 'managing culture' was about an uneven communication process. The top communicated on the level of pathos by norms and values. The employees answered by superficially embracing the transmission, but unofficially responding by irony. The superficiality and speed of organizational ethnography carried out mainly by the use of direct observation have often been criticized (see Susan Wright 1994). Superficiality is indeed a mistake, but organizations tend to be less absorbing cultures than the cultures we are born and socialized into. People have their lives outside the organization. It may not be ideal to study the culture of a social class or a local community by means of direct observation, but, indeed, why not the culture of a workplace, how immersive and tightly managed it claims to be.

Shadowing (Czarniawska-Joerges 2007) is a kind of direct observation that involves a very close relationship between the ethnographer and one of the research participants from the field and is a kind of a mobile observation. The researcher 'shadows', or very closely follows, the organizational activities of a social actor. The social actor performs her social and organizational role but the researcher remains outside of the social structure of the field. Instead, she 'becomes the shadow' of an insider and learns to look at the everyday reality of this person almost from her point of view. At the same time, the ethnographer tries to minimize her presence in the studied situation. It takes some time for the field to accept this extra 'shadow' but once this is done, life tends to go on as if she was not a 'real' social actor. Ulla Johansson (1998) wanted to understand the idea and the practice of responsibility in a Swedish public sector organization. She accompanied a few housing office employees in their everyday work in an attempt to comprehend how they understand their responsibility and how they realized it in practice. She noticed that she was learning by being close to her research participants: not everything they were doing could be expressed verbally, and particularly what it meant in practice for them to 'feel responsible' for someone or something. But she felt a connection thank to the body language and the way her research participants embraced their duties and how they responded to their clients.

3.2   VISUAL ETHNOGRAPHY

BOX 3.2   TO SEE AND TO UNDERSTAND, BY AGATA MORGAN

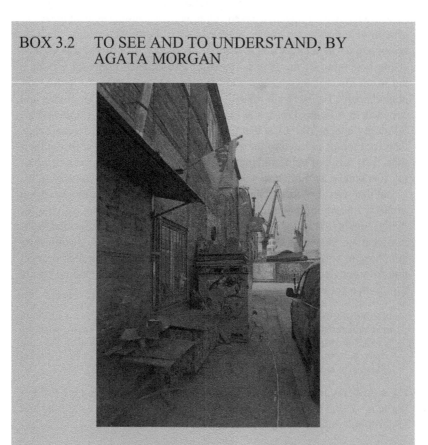

Figure 3.1   Stocznia Gdańska

Photo by Stanisław Zbigniew Kamieński

For several years, I have been returning to the site of the former Gdańsk Shipyard, the place where, in the 1980s, the free trade union Solidarity and the social movement were born out of ordinary human solidarity. In May 2021, I set out again on ethnographic fieldwork, this time together with a few colleagues, trying to investigate what is left of its aura. We want to see, understand and show this, using visual arts-based methods. Artists are said to feel and see more. They are often believed to have some kind of extra sense that allows them to intuit something that only after some time becomes clear and obvious to the rest of society.

A dozen or so years ago, looking up on the wall surrounding the Gdańsk Shipyard, I saw a mural representing Solidarity. From the very first glance I knew what it symbolized: a naked, adult woman standing against the background of the shipyard cranes, which looked like broken wings. She was accompanied by a street dog, a symbol of fidelity. The mural was created at the beginning of the new millennium: the Gdańsk Shipyard was then put in the state of bankruptcy, and there were almost three million unemployed people registered in Poland, who were looking for work in vain and depicted in official statistics as 'high rates of long-term unemployment'. Solidarity appeared to us at that time in the form of an artist, Iwona Zając, who for months listened to the shipyard workers' stories about losing their jobs, their sense of value and meaning in life and then expressed it in a mural. It is known as 'Shipyard Nike' and is a record of Zajac's conversations.

But that was then, study completed, thesis defended. And now, the spring of 2021, I was hoping to see it again and describe it again, not as living (or dying) organizing history but as echoes and reverberances. I decided to invite an artist, Stanisław Zbigniew Kamieński, to work with us. He turned up but chose to walk by himself. I focused on my fieldwork and did not meet him for some days. Then I received some photos from him, including Figure 3.1., with a comment from the author of the photograph:

> In some inconspicuous place, on the wall of a factory building, I saw a flag with the characteristic inscription 'Solidarity'. Actually, if I had not known what the inscription could be, I probably would not have been able to read it; the once white canvas was dirty, tarnished and frayed, twisted many times (by the wind of history?) around the spar.

I was probably in the same place and looking at the same thing but I didn't see *that*. Without art we researchers of the social world feel, would see and understand – less.

Visual ethnography is a type of ethnographic research which is based on intense looking and the sense of seeing. But as the example in Box 3.2 shows, it is much deeper than what is visible. Agata Morgan set out twice to explore the culture of a significant place and twice was struck by a sense of insight and even illumination thanks to an encounter with visual art.

This is due to the cultural significance of the visual. Culture is made up of symbols, which are often of a visual nature, as there has been a strong predominance of the visual dimension in the domain of aesthetics. For many human beings, the sense of sight is central. Some cultural theorists, including the authors of this book, believe that this may be linked to the larger patterns recurrent in human culture, known as archetypes of the collective unconscious (Jung 1981 [1934–1954]), or pre-existing patterns of thought ready to be filled in by visions, images and ideas. Aby Warburg developed an even more explicitly visual notion of such patterns in his Mnemosyne Atlas (2013–2016 [1927]), a kind of visual and metaphoric encyclopaedia: he set out to explore and illustrate how images of great symbolic power emerge throughout time, from antiquity to Weimar Germany. The atlas consists of panels presenting images as they occur and recur in key contexts, such as, for example, how cosmic systems correspond to human harmonies, or heliotropism: visions of the sun and human rituals relating to it. This kind of powerful visual symbolism is so important in understanding human culture, because it enables symbolic work – an ongoing human effort to produce and reproduce individual cultural identities (Willis 1990: 11). According to ethnographer Paul Willis, 'symbolic work includes the selection of objects and items from countless possibilities, and their placement in personal *mises en scene*, in precise micro circumstances, material and symbolic, of use and consumption' (Willis 1990: 72). This kind of work turns human life into an ongoing artwork. Ultimately, ethnographic research needs to be sensitive to and cognizant of this fundamental dimension of living culture. That is why *ethnographic imagination* is of such fundamental importance, or the ability to make connections between everyday life and art in order to make sense of what is observed (Willis 1990: 7). It is about connecting sensual and sensuous meanings with abstract notions and ideas: the very core of symbolic competence. We can see in the example in Box 3.2 how certain symbols need deciphering in order to be fully understood. The philosopher Wolfgang Welsch (1997) considers humans to be particularly endowed for this purpose; as the creators of everyday life (work, free time, identity) the human being is *homo aestheticus*. The aesthetic ethnographic experience, even if primarily of a visual nature, is not purely about seeing, as we shall see in the following section but is invoked through the body; it is an embodied and participative effort at sense-making. Human senses mediate between the internal and external world, so the aesthetic experience is never purely intellectual. For Agata Morgan it became the source of both personal and ethnographic enlightenment. Organization theorist Antonio Strati (1999) emphasizes how the aesthetic dimension is profoundly immersive and omnipresent even in the most profane context of everyday organizational life.

Aesthetic experience comes from a meeting with the material world. Beauty is not subjective (not entirely in the eye of the beholder). Aesthetic judgements are social and 'organizational': to understand social phenomena one has to explore them beyond the purely rational, intellectual surface. Visual ethnography is an approach to ethnographic study aiming to gain such immersive and dynamic understanding.

Sarah Pink, a social anthropologist using visual research methods such as photography, images, video and other media for ethnographic research, argues that the visual is omnipresent, in everyday life as well in ethnographic work. It is a symbolic language connecting the ethnographer and the field, to experience, interpret and present a culture (Pink 2021). For her, it is a method for collecting field material, but also an experiential process. The visual helps to be reflexive, to see ethnographic work as a relationship where something is 'taken' and something 'given'. But it is also a way to *observe the unobservable* (Pink 2021: 23): the 'visual' goes beyond the 'visible' and not everything can be purely recorded or noted down.

Visual ethnography is a way of seeing based on the 'understanding of the significance of the visual in ethnographic work' thanks to 'a reflexive appreciation of how such elements combine to produce visual meanings and ethnographic knowledge' (Pink 2021: 29). It combines methods of studying the cultural context, the affects, emotions and feelings the interactions with the context evoke, as well as the moods and associations that link these two dimensions of ethnographic presence in the field. In actual fieldwork it takes usually one of the three forms (or several combined): observation with the help of visual methods (photographs, sketches), interviews with the help of photos taken by the interviewees, and the creation of and conversation through art. The first use is about using the visual as a kind of ethnographic script, indeed, an *ethno-graphy*; etymologically, the writing of culture by the means of graphic tools of expression. In the words of Samantha Warren:

> Ethnography has always sought to tell richly grounded evocative tales, as we know, but visual methods in particular add another layer to this – they can show others how it feels to work, manage, consume, or otherwise be affected by organizational action, not only to the ethnographer during fieldwork, but via exhibitions, installations, video online and physically. (Warren 2012: 115)

Fieldwork – as shown in the example presented in Box 3.2 – includes capture of pictures, movies, mapping of movement. Such methodological innovations are enabled technological advances which we use in our everyday life, not just for research purposes. Samantha Warren argues that visual ethnographic methods have become more obvious to use, as well as more important, in the era of the mobile phone, digital cameras and social media. However, as the beautiful book *Urban Portraits* (2017) co-created by photographer Keith Moss and organizational ethnographer Robert McMurray shows, collaborative ethnographic work between a researcher and an artist can bring extra depth to the visual material. McMurray is himself a visual ethnographer and the author of beautiful and evocative images,[1] but the collaborative book shows something of the potential of the method not just to communicate symbols but to use them as a means to communicate resonances and subtle moods in the field, bringing forth synergies that are much less dependent on the communicative modes and fashions dependent on the Zeitgeist. Urban Portraits are portraits of individual people as much as of the modern urban setting, as much as of the contemporary way of being in the city. Images are acorns of ethnographical tales that, sometimes, grow and develop into big stories. The ethnographer can take pictures instead of or in addition to ordinary fieldnotes.

The second use of visual methods involves either taking pictures in the field and then discussing them with the participants or asking the participants to take pictures themselves in order to chat about them and their significance. Harriett Shortt and Samantha Warren (2017) argue that a *dialogical* use of visual methods helps to stimulate discussions about everyday life in the field. Ethnographers make choices to take pictures of certain spaces which held a communicative potential that can be explored in discussions with the research participants. The interviewees can also be asked to take photos and these can be used to discuss their meaning (e.g., 'What is this a photo of?', 'Why did you choose to photograph this object?', etc.). But Shortt and Warren recommend going beyond this individual stage and taking all of them together in juxtaposition to each other. Especially valuable is the use of images with a certain common theme or category proposed by the researcher. Then, it is possible to extract 'sedimented social knowledge' (Shortt and Warren 2017: 540) and to pay attention to broader and deeper contextual meanings and see broader symbolic patterns in the material. Both conversation and composition are important: images can generate dialogue with the field and make the voices of the social actors heard in the narratives as well as in the interpretations of the observed symbols. The authors used this method to study the work of hairdressers, of what role space plays in their work experience. They observed salons located in big UK cities during a period of nine months. They also asked their research participants to take 12 images of spaces that were meaningful to them and expressed something important about their work. Then they interviewed the employees, where their images were discussed and analysed together by the ethnographers and the interviewees. Themes were generated from the stories about the photographs and a visual pattern analysis was carried out.

The third use of visual ethnography is focused explicitly on the creation of art, usually by the researcher or by both researcher and researched in a creative dialogue. To some degree this approach was used in Agata Morgan's example (Box 3.2). The relevance of this variation of the method can be traced to the traditional connection between social sciences and art, which, as Antonio Strati (2021) points out, are mutually very strong. On the one hand, art emerges from non-artistic activities and experiences. On the other, social sciences rely on art for much more than just the expression of key ideas; informed by art, social sciences perform a sensitive construction of the social and its visions and understandings. This is due to the relevance of the relationship between the aesthetic dimension and the social ethics. German philosopher and sociologist Harmut Rosa (2019) speaks of *resonance* as an important feature permeating human culture and society: a profound relationship between human beings and their world. It encompasses our biological interchanges with our surroundings, starting with breathing, as well as shared experiences of being a family, doing sports, engaging in religion and much more. Art can help us to understand and express these resonances, as well as co-create them some of them. Art opens up access to the material dimension relating the material context to human experience and life. Polish pedagogical scientist Beata Kunat (2015) believes that all social problems are related to the field of art. Art helps us to see what is fundamental but usually unseen, and, furthermore, it can help both the ethnographer and the research participants to learn reflexively about themselves – and, through that, it is a means of social construction of reality.

Dutch social scientist and artist Terrence Letiche (2021) has carried out an ethnographic study of a public office. As part of his observations and interviews with the employees he created works of art that reflected his findings concerning the resonances he found in two different departments of the institution. He then carried out sessions of discussions dedicated to these artworks, where the research participants talked about how they perceived the art itself as well as their workplace reality, and what the art was able to say about how they felt at work. Throughout the fieldwork he strived at keeping his own ideas about the paintings out of the art he produced, focusing on the stories, moods and reflections of the participants. Finally, based on these sessions, Letiche created a final set of paintings, which served as a personalized artistic conclusion of his study. This time he involved his own feelings and his artistic reflection of the whole topic.

3.3   OTHER SENSES...

Whereas visual ethnography emphasizes seeing and the pictorial, ethnographers know to include all senses in their study because of the multisensorality of human experience: both the researchers' and the researched's (Pink 2009). In Hartmut Rosa's (2019) resonance theory it is hearing that has the strongest significance, but all the senses establish human relationships to the world and all help to absorb and reject, all have a role in the processes of appropriation and assimilation of the world. They activate emotions that prompt how fragments of the world appear to us; fragments that are attractive or dangerous, attractive or repulsive. This is the fabric of human sense-making, an experiential ongoing and embodied process.

BOX 3.3   WHEN I RECALL THAT DAY, I STILL GET A CHILL UP MY SPINE, BY AGNIESZKA CZYCZYŁO

In mid-December 2019, I was conducting a participant observation as part of an ethnography of a project dedicated to the dissemination of ideas and practices of inclusivity and accessibility under the patronage of the Małopolska Institute of Culture. The Sensitive Culture Forum was the crowning event of many months' work. It included, among other things, a series of conferences on accessibility and a concert by the group November Project.

Between the presentations my attention was drawn to the groups of participants talking. Some in sign language, some in English, some held a cane in their hands. I stopped at the back of the room and for the first time in my life I felt that my dreams about accessible places were real. I could actually see people communicating across barriers. And it was happening right in front of me. All the participants know how to behave. What distance to keep to ensure the comfort of the person sitting in the wheelchair. How to speak so that a blind person does not feel surprised by a sudden strange voice. How to convey information to the deaf. During this time I also experienced very strongly how important a role simple gestures play in building accessibility: a shared coffee, small signals that you understand someone, a smile. But all this is built on an awareness of the needs of the person we are with. Dinner at a table where sighted people were a minority drew my attention to the importance of details, the arrangement of cutlery, the choice of words. If only for the moment when my eyes could serve as a culinary guide to what was being served.

In the evening there was a fully accessible concert. It could be experienced using a variety of tools, depending on need: an induction loop, Polish Sign Language translations, audio description, large screen subtitles and backpacks for the Deaf. This solution overcame the last barrier to participation in music that I have known so far. The kits that Deaf people could use consisted of bone conduction headphones, subwoofer speakers and a sound conducting transmitter inside the backpack. Simply put, this apparatus allows you to feel the music. And on stage, phenomenal sign language interpreters conveyed the lyrics with their whole bodies. Their every move, apart from the signs as such, was also a melody. They rose and fell to the rhythm of the songs, they also showed the mood and dynamics. In the bustle of the audience, I saw couples in which one person was deaf. Both dancing, to the rhythm of the same, audible, music. It is a sight incomparable to any other moment of my research. It is a triumph of community in the reception of art.

In addition to the architectural and technical solutions, the diversity of the audience and performers also held an important inclusive aspect. The performers included people with disabilities and the audience included people of all ages, families with children, listeners with different types of disabilities and those without special needs. But interestingly, also directors of institutions, authorities, volunteers and completely unknown participants. A very diverse mix, in which everyone was welcome. No professional hierarchies, divisions or categories.

At the end there was a round of applause, in sign language of course. A crowd of hands raised in the air. I wrote in my thesis:

> I used only qualitative research throughout the work. The organizational realities that interested me, the stories, the interactions between employees, the values they hold dear, the challenges and difficulties of running the project, the philosophy behind Sensitive Culture are themes that would have been impossible to explore with quantitative methods.

One of the key findings of my thesis was that sensitivity and human subjectivity form a core for the resonance of values through which people and organizations can learn and grow. Observing the engagement with which the creators of Sensitive Culture worked to respond to the needs of all participants, staff and volunteers, it was a lovely study for me.

Agnieszka Czyczyło's study presented in Box 3.3 shows the power of observation with the use of all the senses. It not only helps to understand the field in a stronger way, with its different aspects – crucially important in the case of people with disabilities – but also a resonance of the field as such. The senses create synergies that lead to a profoundly poignant and holistic view. Reverberations reveal links between aspects that otherwise may be difficult to see let alone to grasp. These links influence sensitivities and values. There are many interesting examples of sense-based ethnographies, of which we present the following selection meant as inspiration for the reader's own quests and pursuits rather than as a summary.

Organizational theorists Tommy Jensen and Johan Sandström have been engaging in an ethnographic project aimed at the exploration of power relations and labour processes in the mining industry. They realized almost immediately, upon entering the field, how much of the work in the mine can be understood through the sense of hearing. The result is a musical project,

Organizing Rocks (Jensen and Sandström 2019), which combines poetry, rhythm and rock music to make sense of and express the material they have collected through observation and interviews. Their recent book (Jensen and Sandström 2021) is a written reflection embracing all their research experiences, including a narrative of the aural dimension of the project: from the organization of work to the machinery and technology involved, what their research participants say but also how their voices sound. This also leads to a sense of coming into the realization of deeper and usually hidden reverberations between values, conflicts and power.

The importance of smell has perhaps become more evident during the Covid-19 pandemic, when a number of people fell ill and temporarily lost their smell and taste. Philosophers have known (even if not always appreciated) for a long time how vividly important it is for humans. Chantal Jaquet (2010) is one among them who does both – she develops a philosophy of the nose. The anthropological discovery can be made by olfactory sensibility, and it also helps to construct memory and affectivity, as well as identity and alterity. Kat Riach's and Sam Warren's (2015) ethnography of smell concerns everyday smells in workplaces, such as UK offices. They talked about smells with their research participants and they kept own observation diaries of smell. The study led them to reflections on the interconnection of shared, personal, local and cultural elementals of office smells, as something located in-between other symbols and experiences. Smell marks connectedness of the most spontaneous and embodied kind: the feeling of being present together, in a familiar space.

Taste is a related sense, and similarly embodied and localized. Carole Counihan and Susanne Højlund (2018) present ethnographies of social relations shaped by and through the taste of food. Cultures are often associated with different cuisines and tastes for food. Taste experiences and preferences can reveal how cultural differences are generated, and how collective identity is shaped. Taste is strongly valued and there is much going on around it that permeates education and socialization. The book is as much about food and taste as about talking about food, which is an important part of human everyday experience. How do we share taste, why is it so important? Taste is subjective but a strong ingredient in community building. It is also territorialized: food is connected to *terroir*, it expresses the uniqueness of the place where it is grown and prepared.

Just as with smell and taste, we became more aware of the sense of touch during the lockdowns. Richard Kearney's (2021) book on touch was much discussed during seminars and as part of (online) book circles. Our increased reliance on online work and study brought on a wave of sensory deprivation and the readers tended to agree with Kearney's claim that we are in danger of losing touch with each other and ourselves in the times of increased virtual presence. A vital aspect of touch is interdependence: it is a reciprocal sense, and one which we are not able to control. However, as we were made aware during the pandemic, it has a power of bringing people together, it has the potential of bringing a literally tangible sense of community and pleasure of belonging. Emmanouela Mandalaki and Mar Pérezts (2020) ethnographically explore dance. In an article dedicated to tango, they explore how dance offers inter-corporeality as a phenomenological experience and invokes the transformational potential of eros. Knowledge is embodied and erotic – something which is easy to forget in rationalistic discourse but which the experience of dance makes not just central but evident. Such *being-in-and-with-the-field* experiences can help us to reclaim 'the transformational potential of our inter-corporeal encounters to create new possibilities for dancing, living, loving, researching and writing together in academia' (Mandalaki and Mar Pérezts 2020: 19).

Proprioception is also a firmly embodied sense: of movement, gravity, and space. Organization theorist Heather Höpfl often used ethnographic methods and modes of reflection to understand the relationship between humans and space in organizational settings. In one of her texts (Höpfl 2002) she adopts the metaphor of vertigo to present the construction of the sublime in the process of organizing. The study of the kinetic sphere helps to perceive and understand the melancholy of commodified representations of organizational idealization, which is represented in strategies in organizational change as something abstract and rational, but which also has an important embodied aspect of an obsessive-compulsive pursuit. The ethnographer perceives it as distance and about movement: the underpinning of the theatrical sublimation of organizational roles as they unravel. Dance can also be experienced as movement and, since Edward Evans-Pritchard (1928), has been considered a topic for anthropological study. Helena Wulff's (2020) intensive study of dance and choreography presents different aspects of work of famous ballet companies, including the intense backstage experiences of fatigue, stress and pain that are transformed into weightlessness in onstage performance. Dance ethnography is immersive: the ethnographer takes part in the dancing, and acquires access to embodied special knowledge which is accessible only through participation.

As in the example in Box 3.3, these studies show something at the same time embodied and profound; connections that extend beyond the individual and form a fabric of togetherness, sociality or, indeed, organizing itself.

NOTE

1.　　We wholeheartedly recommend taking a look at his 'visual ethnographic notebook' in the form of the blog: http://robertmcmurray.blogspot.com/

4. Talking and listening

4.1 THE INTERVIEWEE

Our colleague, considering himself a positivist, once asked one of us how is it possible that the research participants, all very busy people, first refused to take part in his questionnaire studies on the grounds of not having enough time, and then devoted several hours to her ethnographic interviews. It was a rather interesting situation, because, at this time, we actually tried to persuade the same people to take part in our different studies.[1] The collision was real enough and several of the very same persons who could not take part in questionnaire research gladly did in the ethnographic study. But no tricks or special abilities were involved – it is something quite different happened here, we think. People *give* their scarce time to the quantitative researcher equipped with a questionnaire. But they both give *and* take time from the ethnographer. The qualitative interview is a two-way communication: the researcher takes field material from the interview but gives back something really valuable – interest and attention. The ability to listen, to be present face to face is precious. The ethnographer is a good and dedicated listener: the interlocutor can allow herself hesitation, experimenting with thoughts, expressing ambivalence and uncertainty; all without any practical consequences. The research participants, perhaps especially so when they are responsible for an organization or community, such as managers, do not have many such listeners in their everyday organizational life. Even in their free time they are probably not likely to find anyone willing to listen for hours to them 'talking job'.

BOX 4.1   MEETING THE STREET ARTISTS, BY MARTA POŁEĆ

From 2012 to 2019, I conducted ethnographic research focused on the informal activities of street artists in Polish cities. During this time, I got to know many street performers and I saw some of them many times over the years. For some of them, my first reappearance might have come as a surprise, but later they learned both to know me better and what ethnography was all about. So it became rather expected to see me again and again, and, in a sense, I started to be recognized as someone belonging to the community.

But thinking back to the beginnings – how did I initiate the interviews? When conducting field research in urban spaces, I always took the opportunity to first see an artist perform. This way, based on the interaction with the audience, I could assume whether the artist would be interested in participating in my research at all and how I should approach them. The performance was also a kind of an illumination for me about what to say: during the observation, questions related to the performances came to my mind. If I decided to meet someone, I always introduced myself as a researcher and talked about my research. I tried to talk for a while about the performances and only then set up an interview. The interviews were casual, so in order to find out about the street artists' activities, I wanted above all to find out about their personal stories and the themes they considered important. I usually left the choice of venues for the interviews to the interviewees, so I was able to get to know their favourite cafés or neighbourhoods in the urban space where they felt comfortable, which undoubtedly contributed to the atmosphere of the conversation.

I felt that it was easy to make friends and establish relationships with street artists because they were generally open-minded people and showed me much kindness because of my interest in their work. Many of my interlocutors were more or less my age. However, even where there was a greater age difference, the artists tended to prefer direct contact. Owing to their independent way of performing in urban spaces, I did not need to officially gain access to the research area. I have always treated my interviewees exceptionally, giving my full attention to them and their concerns, and making every effort to be impartial, verbal and discreet in my dealings with the artist community. Had it not been for the disinterested help of my interviewees, for which I tried to repay with photographs, invitations to coffee or simply affection, I probably would not have been able to obtain their unique accounts of a reality so little known.

An interview is not a free exchange of views, but, rather, a situation where the interviewee offers narratives on topics that are of interest to the researcher. It is a kind of conversation which is driven by a specific purpose, but nonetheless is a reciprocal and mutual interaction (Gudkova 2018). People offer interpretations of their world in interviews, not 'facts' or 'data'. The person of the interviewee and her world, even if usually not 'leading' the conversation, are central to this ethnographic method. Svetlana Gudkova points out that the interview is an 'interaction which takes place between two persons who form their experiences and interpretations of their past behavior together' (Gudkova 2018: 77).

In ethnographic research, the interaction is part of a long term process. As in Marta Połeć's vignette (Box 4.1), the relationship between the ethnographer and the interviewee developed intensively over time. A quality that is fundamental for this development is trust. It is absolutely crucial to acquire it and, once attained, care to maintain it. Trust is difficult to build up and easy to destroy. Maintaining confidentiality of the interview is a necessary first condition. Another important point of departure is the way we treat our interviewees. Ethnographers do not call them 'respondents', because they do much more than just respond. They are partners and helpers of the researcher, rather than passive informants. Evidently, we should take great care about their voice not being misrepresented in the produced text that results from the research (Fontana and Frey 1994). Respect is due not just during the face-to-face interactions but throughout the entire ethnographic process. But there is more than that involved.

It is also important to consider where the interview is to take place. On the one hand, interviewing people in their own context, such as in the workplace, is very informative, because the interview is also an occasion to observe (Czarniawska 2014). But sometimes it is good to find another place, more private and relaxed, such as a café. Such semi-private meetings can be a good ground for the development of trust. Marta Połeć held her initial interviews with the street artists in the streets of the cities where they worked and nearby cafés. Later on, as their mutual relationships were developing, and she gained their trust and sometimes also friendship, they met and talked in a number of places, including the homes of the interviewees. Her relationships with the research participants developed in different contexts, over time, as well as in different places. She became a recognizable person in her field. She herself got to recognize and understand a large number of aspects and dimensions of her field.

Another question concerns whom to interview. Usually one person is interviewed by one interviewer. However, sometimes the conversation is not just about experiences and ideas of the interlocutor but when group dynamics or communication is of interest. Then a group interview is the way to go (Fontana and Frey 1994). Andrea Fontana and James Frey stress how important it is for the interviewer to adapt to the world of the interlocutors and try to share their concerns and outlooks, particularly when dealing with coherent groups. Only by doing so can he or she learn anything at all.

And yet there is problem in the ways of communication as such. Language is important on many levels in ethnographic research: as an object of study, as a medium for communication of the research, as well as the way to communicate with the field. These areas are not separate. Anthropologists studying faraway cultures learn the language of their research participants. The social or organizational ethnographer usually does not need to learn foreign languages, although it does happens at times when the researcher heads for the field located abroad. But even in one's own cultural context it can be important to be sensitive toward dialects, jargons and slang. It may turn out that a key word that the researcher takes for granted has a totally different meaning in the field being studied, or is not used at all. Karin Winroth (1999) observed that the word *management*[2] was used in a particular way in the law firm she was studying. This discovery led her to some important insights concerning not just the culture of the organization she was studying, but some of its organizing principles. This would not have happened if she had ignored the idiosyncratic subtleties in the way the research participants used the word. But there is more to it than just sensitivity: she avoided imposing her taken-for-granted diction-ary on her field. Ethnographers are often weary – rightfully so – of 'infecting' the field with their own language. Such linguistic disruptions can happen quite unintentionally and even unconsciously, due to the way the researcher asks her questions. Insisting on a particular word or just being a cool person using a certain phrase can be enough to alter the way the field is communicating.

4.2   SHORTER INTERVIEWS

We have titled this section 'shorter interviews' although not necessarily in the sense of 'interviews of short duration' or 'fast interviews'. Some interviews regularly used by ethnographers are 'shorter' in that they do not require long-term relationships or commitment to the field. The heart of ethnographic work is about the building of relationships, talking with the 'natives', coming back to the same interviewees with new questions and conversations. But sometimes a 'shorter' engagement will do, not as the main method to employ, but a supporting way of gaining additional insight.

BOX 4.2   READING CHANGES IN-BETWEEN THE
           LINES: LIBRARIES DURING A PANDEMIC,
           BY MACIEJ GODOŚ, KAROLINA OLEKSY
           AND BARTOSZ WOJTASZEK

The lockdowns were, finally, over, we were able to meet in person. So we did that to think together and talk about possible topics for our project. Among many things that interested us, finally the idea to study libraries during the pandemic emerged and gained more and more power of attrac-tion. What was it like to work as a librarian in these unusual times? Were there any changes in the way these organizations worked and, if so, how did these changes affect the employees? We were curious how the restrictions affected both the people working every day among books and silence, as well as the readers. Were they able to look for the knowledge hidden in the books on the shelves, or did they turn to the virtual collections they were holding?

The first call was not answered, so we called again. And then again, and again. Finally, a voice came from the other side: 'Good morning, I have been waiting impatiently for this call'. Our interlocutor said he was fascinated by the possibility of talking to us ever since he found out about our research (from an email correspondence). He wanted us to use his real name in the report, but this we could not do. An ethnographer takes care not to reveal the identity of his or her interviewees. We met him and the conversation was enthralling. In many details, in a beautiful flowing language, he drew us a picture of the library of which he was director. He told about the successive stages of implementing the restrictions related to the pandemic. They were fascinating and expressed in smooth narratives.

Our next interviewee, also a librarian, was less enthusiastic about our research. During our first visit to her library, she refused to participate in the study. She referred to the need to obtain written permission from the management. We were observed by other library staff. They excitedly passed on information to each other about what was happening. After a tedious email correspondence, the management finally agreed to the study. We arranged an online interview with our interviewee. She pondered each question. But this time she did not ignore us: she took the interview very seriously. Carefully and succinctly, she gave us an overview of the operation of her branch during the pandemic. However, she left us with huge dissatisfaction, because we felt that the conversation was merely formal, no bond was forged and we never spoke to her again.

Our third interviewee surpassed our expectations. Not only did she invite us into a safe space, specially prepared for an in-person meeting, but she was full of empathy, understanding for our research, she gave us the information we needed, highlighting the most important points. It was a splendid interview on many levels, including the personal.

All of our interlocutors gave us knowledge and information which we collated and turned into conclusions. It turned out, to our surprise, that everyone quickly came to terms with the new rules, and the introduction of these rules did not discourage readers from making use of the treasure trove of novels, novellas, volumes of poetry and scientific books. The main problem was the lack of a real encounter with readers and the longing for the interpersonal relationships they built. Thanks to technology, the link between readers and librarians did not break, and it was possible to stay in touch. But it made a difference to be able to meet in person: just as it did for us.

The project described in Box 4.2 is a brief study aimed as part of a course in (qualitative) research methods. It did not extend beyond short inquiries. Yet it brought some genuinely interesting material to think of and discuss in class. Given the time and need, it could have been supplemented by longer interviews and observations and then grown into a full-size ethnography. Sometimes brief interviews like the ones used by the students can give something quite valuable for an ethnographer: a glimpse of the human diversity of the field, the different viewpoints, temperaments, experiences. It can be a really good thing to do a first short study like this one before entering the field more intensively, in order to gain preliminary insight about whom to interview and what to talk about. These accounts can be either solicited or unsolicited; as in everyday life, people converse constantly and tell each other what had happened and why (Hammersley and Atkinson 2019). Ethnographers can actively ask for explanations and accounts (as in the example in Box 4.2) or just be there taking part in conversations or overhearing them.

Short solicited interviews are usually semi-structured, as in the example from the student's project. The researcher has some questions he wishes to ask, either as a reaction to what is happening in the field or after consideration. This can help him to compare different responses coming from a number of interviewees or relate their accounts to a situation observed in the field. The character of ethnographic research does not necessitate a close 'sticking to the script' or list of questions – on the contrary, it rather precludes it. A list can be prepared but spontaneous responses are welcome, especially those providing context (Kostera and Modzelewska, 2021). It is also important to take good care to observe and note everything that accompanies the accounts, no matter how unimportant or accidental it seems, in particular all nonverbal elements of the conversation: such shorter interviews are an excellent way of gaining more material to frame the spoken words (Fontana and Frey 1994).

Research participants sometimes venture unsolicited explanations, to counter what the researcher may believe or infer (Hammersley and Atkinson 2019). This may happen in particular during the initial phases of an ethnographic project, when the social actors of the field are not yet familiar with the researcher. This is an excellent opportunity to gather such additional clarifications and it does the study well to be attentive to such occasions when they occur.

Unsolicited interviews as methods providing ethnographic material can be used and interpreted in at least two ways. First, they bring content stemming from the field, just like longer interviews. The students preparing a project on libraries (Box 4.2) welcomed additional explanations from the librarians and used them exactly as they used the material from the formal and purposeful interviews with them. Second, the data can be analysed as observation material. It is a good idea to note which voices from the field are spontaneous and which responses to the researcher's questions. It is in itself interesting to see which information was volunteered by the interviewees and in what context, what promoted them to offer it. The statements as such can also be used as a kind of received material and analysed from the point of view of its form. A method of analysis that can be used for this purpose is conversation analysis based on the ethno-methodological tradition (Silverman 1993). It focuses on how conversations between social actors in their various social roles are constructed, which figures of speech and behaviours constitute the way of playing a role in the field. In other words it is about *how* people say things rather than *what* they say. The content of the interview is read from the perspective of society, place and time. There exists a whole set of rules and methods for how to apply a specific script that enables such reading (Silverman 1993), but in ethnographic research it is less important that all these rules are closely followed. The study may contain elements of rigorous conversation analysis as described by David Silverman but does not necessarily have to. It is more important to focus on an analysis of how the statements of the research participants relate to other people and to elements of their social and organizational roles. All details of a conversation: the language, jargon, intonation, turns of phrase, breaks and their duration, words inserted as a kind of 'punctuation' can be interesting and valid interview material. For example, the example in Box 4.2 shows how the interviewees react to the presence of the researchers. Their first interlocutor uses a very polite phrase to greet the students, at the same time personalizing the interaction. The second interviewee, however, makes it clear that she needs a formal guideline and spoke to them in a more formal, businesslike language.

4.3   THE LONG (OPEN) INTERVIEW

Very often, ethnographers do not differentiate between diverse types of interviews. They do not encapsulate fluid and contingent ways of talking with people into formal categories because most valuable interactions in the field are intense, often spontaneous, and informal. It is instrumental in knowing the types of interviews described above and their characteristics to implement them when needed. However, an ethnographic project does not require us to specify upfront which interviews we will use and in which quantity unless an external force, such as a grant giving body, needs it.

It may be helpful to understand the specificity of interviews and other forms of listening in ethnography through the comparison with interviews used in broader qualitative research. Even if formal and scheduled upfront, ethnographic interviews are rarely conducted outside the natural context of the people, while, often, Individual In-depth Interviews (IDI) or Focus Group Interviews (FGI) are performed in out-of-the-context spaces in the laboratory settings. An interview's in-field location allows researchers to ask about physical artefacts spotted in the field. We can even structure a conversation around an object or the surroundings. Any element of the area can become an inspiration to ask a question. Embodied experience, emotions, observed interactions, or even what is uncertain is a good conversation topic. This is why I, Paweł, was, whenever possible, trying to get to the Siberian taiga and on the river with my research participants and talk about hunting, fishing and the woods there and not just be sitting in the house. The tools such as fishing nets, the way they were checked, and the body language while the local fisherman navigated the boat on the river, gave inspiration for questions and topics that the ethnographer could ask the local guide to narrate.

Another characteristic typical of ethnographic interviewing is the relationship we develop with research participants. Some interviews are a series of conversations while working together, eating and playing. It allows us to continue the conversations, raising new topics. In addition, it changes the nature of discussions as the relationship transforms from that of a stranger to more friend-like, with all the complex consequences of that process.

Formal interviews with a clear start and finish allow the research participants to easily define the situation as participating in research. However, whereas ethnographers may start asking questions over dinner or a drink, the definition of the situation is not always completely clear anymore. Moreover, after a prolonged time spent in the field, ethnographers may become friends with those they came to study. Therefore, constant reflexivity and ethical awareness is necessary for ethnographers. Sometimes ethnographers decide not use some parts of material even if formally they acquired an informed consent. Still, they may feel that a specific bit of information was shared in a heartfelt moment, and rather in their role as friend, not a researcher. Perhaps releasing the material would harm or undermine trust, not only in this particular relation but also in ethnographers and academic researchers. Then it is sound ethnographic practice not to pass this information on.

Research participants may identify themselves in the text despite a careful anonymization of individuals' identities in written monographs. It may be advisable to delete all such potential revelations from the published text. However, one would also keep in mind that the typical reaction to one's own words in a manuscript is a feeling of awkwardness to reading quotes transcribed verbatim, even if interlocutors know that nobody will link these words with the participants.

American writer and Pulitzer Prize winner John Marquand captured, in one of his books, this uncomfortable feeling of reading ethnography involving details about someone's life. In his novel *Point of no Return*, Marquand describes the life of the same town in New England as a field site for anthropologist Lloyd Warner. The fiction writer depicted the anthropologist in the novel as one of the leading characters. An exciting moment of the story depicts the situation when the main protagonist, who was born and raised in the town where the ethnographic fieldwork took place, opens *Yankee Persepolis*, the book written by the anthropologists about the social organization of the city. In this academic monograph, he reads the following passage:

> Charles turned to the middle of the book. Even that quick perusal brought him back to the time when Malcolm Bryant had been studying Yankee Persepolis. He could remember Malcolm's voice and Malcolm's alien figure on the main street, but it was curiously shocking to find that period preserved in print.
>
> 'Typical of a lower-upper family,' Charles was reading, 'are the Henry Smiths— father, mother, son and daughter. Like other lower-upper families, they dwell on a side street ('side streeters'), yet are received on Mason Street...'
>
> Charles felt his face redden, because it was easy enough to read between the lines. It was his own family there in black and white, starkly indecent, without trimming or charity. He was Tom, that likable young graduate from Dartmouth. It was indecent and infuriating, but he still read further.
>
> 'Let us examine a typical day in the Smith family (lower-upper). The rising hour is seven. Tom starts the coal fire in the kitchen range. Mrs. Smith arises to prepare breakfast, the maid Martha Brud (middle-lower) not appearing until eight. Hannah does not assist at this function because of a parental effort, very marked in the lower-upper and continuing through the middle group, for social advancement, especially of the marriageable daughter. The distinction in this regard between son and daughter seems definitely marked.'
>
> There it was in black and white, devoid of tone and shading, but Charles could see the rest between the lines. He could remember Malcolm coming in to call and talking of the Orinoco River and even helping with the dishes and giving his father an Overland cigar. He might have called it pacifying the head man, and he must have rushed to his notebook before he could forget.
>
> 'The ancestral motif is as marked in this group as it is in the upper-upper. The same importance is attached to the preservation of the heirloom and the decoration of the grave. Thus over the mantel of the Smith parlor is jealously guarded a primitive oil painting of a sailing vessel captained by the Smiths' ancestor, Jacob Smith.'
>
> He could clearly recall Malcolm's interest in that picture and the satisfaction in his mother's voice as she had explained it to him. He himself owned the picture now and every word he read seemed to him a crude breach of hospitality. (Marquand 1949: 58)

What Charles read in the monograph were extensive details of material derived from the ethnographer's material gathered during meetings with his own family. Back then, as a young boy, Charles perceived the researcher's visits as friendly, but now, when described in an ethnography, they turned into something less pleasant, something of a breach of hospitality. Somehow the warm and personal researcher clashed with the more distanced and interpreting author. For some students this may pose a problem. One of Monika's students felt so loyal to her field that she refused to discuss her material from any other standpoint than the research participants' – the employees of a musical radio station. She was trying to erase her own ideas and preconceptions from the study so much that she practically refrained from asking questions at all, instead engaging in close to informal conversations. She took everything the field told her very seriously and even as literally valid. During the presentation of her thesis, she became tearful at one moment, when a reviewer asked a question expressing some doubt as to the intentions of the social actors she cited. She defended the sincerity of her field and invoked engaged ethnography (Behar 1993) – a way of doing ethnography that aims at coming as close to the perspective of the field as possible. Despite her lack of distance, the project was considered a valuable ethnographic account.

But being 'too personal' is not the only possible problem of the interviewer. During his first ethnographic project, one of our students was returning from the field every day, frustrated with the low quality of interviews he had conducted. His conversations with people were concise, answers to his questions very brief and often unfinished. Paweł decided to accompany the student one day into the field. The first seconds of the interview made clear that the problem was not in the introverted nature of the student, as he initially had thought. It was instead a technical one. The student had written down all the questions, formulated a list of entire sentences, and he was reading the questions from the document. The consequences were unfavourable for the quality of the interview. Reading questions distanced both parties involved in this interaction. First, written language is formal and imposes a rigid situation. Second, looking at the list of questions, one is losing eye contact with the research participant. Third, the student followed the predesigned question sequence instead of following the logic of evolving conversation. The successful solution to this problem was simple. Paweł asked the student to write a brief interview guide composed of only discussion topics, the keywords, not full sentences. The student was then asked to converse with people without looking at this document. Only at the end of the interaction was he to consult the guide to see if any crucial topics had not been covered.

In fact, ethnographic interviews may use a full spectrum of directness. As in the example of Paweł's student, the initial high degree of interview formalization may result in receiving answers people give to outsiders. In the worst-case scenario, the interrogated person would provide brief answers to reach the end of the interview as soon as possible. Monika's student received responses that were probably expressions of deep trust but she did little to interpret them or even place them in relationship to other information she obtained.

Taking all this into the consideration, it may be something of a sound rule of thumb that asking direct questions about the topic the ethnographer is interested in may not be a good idea. In his classic monograph *Street Corner Society*, William Foote Whyte describes one lesson that Doc, his key informant, the local gang leader, gave him. When visiting a former important gambling operator who was about to tell them about the organization of illegal activities, the ethnographer was too direct in asking and commenting on the story they were listening to. In response, the former gambling operator switched to a conversation about another more neutral topic. Whyte felt uncomfortable for the rest of the day. Only the next day Doc explained to him what had happened and gave an essential lesson on the ethnographic method

> Go easy on that 'who', 'why', 'when', 'where' stuff. You ask those questions, and people will clam up on you. If people accept you, you can just hang around, and you'll learn the answer in the long run without even having to ask a question. (Whyte 1993 [1943]: 303)[3]

After this event, Whyte sat and listened to his interlocutors more attentively than before and recognized that he had learned answers to questions he would not have had. When Whyte acquired a more established position in the local society, he recollected that 'the data came to me without very active efforts on my parts' (Whyte 1993 [1943]: 304). Only then, when Whyte had some particular topics that he would like to explore, could he more easily organize and conduct more formal interviews than at the beginning of being in the field. This methods lesson from the research participant has formed several generations of ethnographers, as the *Street Corner Society* ethnography became a canonical reading for sociology, anthropology and organizational studies students seven decades ago, and is still in use.

How ethnographers approach conversations with research participants depends on the characteristics of the field, and on the researchers' theoretical perspective. We believe in a holistic approach to ethnography – to us, ethnography is more than a method. It is integrated with the lenses through which a researcher perceives and interprets the world. Therefore interviewing is more than data gathering – it is the building of relationships. However, in some rare cases, ethnographic interviewing is just a fact-gathering tool.

The ethnographic approach has been influenced by the narrative turn, which made the objective fact a problematic and uncomfortable concept (see for example Goodall 2000). Quite often, ethnographers do not take what people say at face value (unless they do engaged ethnography), not because they do not trust research participants but because of deeper ontological and epistemological assumptions. Research on emotions in organizations can be an excellent example of how such assumptions and the theoretical perspective may influence how we conduct interviews and work with conversation-based data. Ethnographers interested in emotions would approach conversations during fieldwork depending on the theoretical framework they use to make sense of the emotions as a phenomenon. There is a strong perspective that emotions are socially constructed or a discourse focuses on narrations only.

They can even work with interview data similar to written utterances, such as social media discussions, poetry, and documents. But there are also other views on emotions which recognize the crucial aspect of embodied experience, biological and ecological processes that cannot be reduced to being socially constructed. In this case, what research participants say in interviews and other conversations allows us to learn about the translation of bodily experience into socially recognizable expressions. This second group of researchers may be more attentive to the interlocutors' physical expressions and interactions with the environment.

Sometimes the field allows only for a particular type of interview and inter-action with research participants. For example, sometimes interviews are part of participant observation when the researcher's control over the exchange is and should be limited. In contrast, ethnographers doing direct observation are often quite flexible when it comes to whom and how to interview.

Numerous contingencies shape the final result of how a conversation with research participants unfolds. Because ethnographers are not distancing themselves from the studied groups through highly codified research tools, they have to confront and make sense of dynamic and incoherent reality constantly escaping their interpretations. As a result, we are continually looking for new and better ways of grasping reality through ethnographic interviews. We believe that most ethnographers would agree that researchers are free to explore diverse interviewing approaches unless they are attentive to the possible consequences of their choices.

When it comes to reading and interpreting of interview material, there is at least as great a diversity of approaches as to the interviewing process. There is no one way ethnographers approach empirical data gathered through interviews. It depends, likewise, on the phenomenon under study and the theoretical perspective. It ranges from deeper context-independent ontological assumptions, from social constructivism to idealism, and depends on considerations connected to the context and research questions.

Let's consider two extreme ends of the spectrum: positivism and constructivism. Being a contemporary ethnographer and having a positivist perspective on interviewing is unlikely. Positivists perceive researchers as neutral actors extracting facts from a respondent and gaining access to reality this way. They would probably not use ethnography as a research method as it would be hard to meet standards of being neutral and objective in the way positivism understands it. Positivist interviews emphasize control over the interaction to neutralize the researcher's impact through standardized questions and interview structure. Social constructivism was for several decades a popular vantage point for many ethnographers. Those ethnographers embraced the dialogical aspect of interviewing. The meaning was created and discovered in the researcher and research participant interaction. This approach is in line with Holstein and Gubrium's (1997: 123) *active interviewing*, which aims at providing 'an environment conducive to the production of the range and complexity of meanings that address relevant issues, and not be confined to predetermined agendas'. Hence, the level of the researcher's control over the flow of the interview is minimal. The aims of interviewing, the degree of the researcher's control over the interview, and the way we generalize based on interview data depend on a researcher's theoretical approach. The two contrasting and extreme perspectives result in quite different interviewing practices. Positivist interviewing is more controlling, extracting facts about objectively existing reality and trying to make broader generalizations based on empirical data. The social constructivist approach, in turn, requires less control, to be open to accessing interviewees' perspectives, and even to recognize a researcher's active involvement in creating the social reality. The researcher focuses on the narratives and tries to interpret them using a theoretical lens. As a result, the generalizations based on such empirical material should be local. The opposition between positivism and social constructivism is a clear and useful framework for thinking about interviewing but is not by no means exhaustive. Researchers actively look for theories and develop them in their academic mission. Those ontological, epistemological and even axiological assumptions influence how we approach interviewing.

For example critical realism is an approach in-between these extreme positions. Critical realists apply a layered ontology perspective, making them more willing to control the interview process. They may even approach the field with some theory-driven hypothesis about how broader structural and cultural forces shape individual behaviour, which may seem rather far from what a traditional ethnographic approach to interviewing should be like. However, the openness to a personal perspective makes this approach compatible with ethnographic interviewing.

Finally, the role of the researcher can be more or less dominant or self-effacing. Are ethnographers allowed talk about themselves, or should they limit their activities to asking questions and listening to the answers? We are interchangeably calling an ethnographic interview a conversation because it is an exchange, as with any other conversation. This characteristic differentiates it from interrogation. First, an obvious type of exchange happens when the research participant is also interested in our country, culture, and organization. Sharing some stories that would be valuable for the interviewee is something we can give back. Conversation can also be viewed as a collective meaning and knowledge production (Gudkova 2018). An interview seen as a meeting of two worldviews requires a dialectical approach, where even a disagreement can finally arrive at some synthesis. A joke from Esther Newton's article reminds us to keep the balance and remember that we are going to the field to learn from the field.

> A post-modern anthropologist and his informant are talking; finally, the informant says, 'Okay, enough about you, now let's talk about me.' (Newton 1993: 3)

A meaningful gift the interviewer can offer in exchange to what the interviewee says is to listen carefully to her, with attention and empathy.

BOX 4.3   BETWEEN 'EMIC' AND 'ETIC': A COMMUNITY TELLS THEIR OWN STORY, BY AGNIESZKA KOSIOROWSKA

The structure of an academic paper, a grant proposal, or a dissertation seems to suggest that the work of an ethnographer is composed of neatly separable work packages. One comes up with a topic, research questions and hypothesis, finds and reads relevant literature, and then finally goes to the field and back home to write one's paper. Anthropology's long tradition of undertaking overseas journeys to study the so-called 'simple societies' contributes to maintaining the illusion that 'emic' can easily be distinguished from 'etic', and gathering data and interpreting it with expert knowledge are two different things. As is often the case, in reality, things turn out to be much more confusing.

During the one year I spent in Paris as an exchange student. I decided to do fieldwork in a Polish migrant community in the city. I was interested in transmitting language and cultural identity from Polish mothers to children. I made it part of my weekly routine to frequent various Polish institutions, such as a Polish church or the Polish Library in Paris. This strategy put me in the way of not only regular church-goers and book-seekers but also numerous local experts – librarians, teachers, writers, artists, clergy and academics – all with strong opinions about what a young researcher like myself should read and what are the subjects worth writing about when one studies this community.

Before I started my research, I believed that the Polish migrant community in Paris was understudied. And now I was frequently asked about authors I knew nothing about or introduced to scholars convinced that I must know their works by heart. Naturally, I started familiarizing myself with the literature I was expected to know. At first, I found it very hard to apply it to my work. The work I was reading was heavily anchored in a romantic national tradition. I soon understood that the only topics considered worthy of undertaking were those related to nineteenth-century Polish political exiles, national heroes and romantic artists who found refuge in Paris, their descendants, or institutions which maintained their legacy. Those who lived and worked in Paris today were hidden in the shadow of the great founding fathers of the 'Polish Paris', whose names are known to every child back in Poland: Adam Mickiewicz, Fryderyk Chopin... I understood that my interlocutors – not only the 'experts' but many others – don't want me to write about their daily struggles but about the heroic past of their community.

To navigate my field (and be treated seriously), I had to become well acquainted with the legacy of the nineteenth-century exiles. Yet, I was still resolved to study contemporary Polish women and the unpaid work they were voluntarily involved in, bringing up bilingual children. Only now, I better understood their motives – like them, I was now immersed in a romanticized myth of the 'Polish Paris', surrounded by institutions which upheld it. I realized that the expert knowledge that the Polish community in Paris produced shaped the social reality in which my fieldwork took place and that, to write about this community, I had to build upon what they had already said about themselves. I also understood that through insisting that I should be interested in the nineteenth-century migrants, their contemporary counterparts were negotiating how an outsider may write about them – and I knew I had to take this seriously.

NOTES

1. But not the other way around – possibly due to the much smaller number of interviewees needed in the ethnographic study than in the questionnaire.
2. In English in the original Swedish book.
3. Book originally published in 1943.

5. Reading and writing

5.1 TEXT ANALYSIS

Ethnographers exploring organizations and most social communities do not only observe and talk with people, but, for many reasons, they usually also read and analyse a large variety of texts stemming from the field. Many contemporary social organizations are great text producers, be it in printed form, or, even more copiously, on the internet. The form and style of these texts differ quite a lot, as do their intended readership and their aim. Texts such as annual reports, prospectuses, organizational charts, internal regulations, bulletins, announcements, advertisements, blogs, zines, community newspapers, etc., call for different approaches and engagements. There is a large number of possible methods to choose from for the ethnographer, such as culture analysis, rhetorical analysis and semiotic analysis, poststructuralist analysis, gender analysis, content analysis, and much more. We will not present them all in this chapter, as the intention of this book is not to provide a complete manual but to serve as a guide to ethnographic work in the field. Therefore, we will focus on some aspects of texts produced in the field which may be relevant for most ethnographers, such as author and reader, means of communication, and context.

Ethnographers can read texts deriving from the field at least in two main modes (Eco 1990): the semantic and semiotic. The semantic reader is a 'naïve' reader, one who follows with its flow and allows the text to guide her. The semiotic reader is a reflective and critical reader, deliberating both what the text says and *how* it says it; why the text is experienced as invoking certain moods, feelings and ideas. The ethnographer may look both for the communicative dynamics as well as the hidden aspects, and how the text has an impact on the reader.

Who is the author of the text and who the intended reader? Italian philosopher's Umberto Eco's ideas of textual strategies (1989 [1962]) may come in useful for dealing with these issues, central for the understanding of a text's communicative potential. The model reader is not the same as the empirical reader but the type of reader can depend on the way the text is constructed, in order to have it read in a certain manner. The intentions of the text correspond with the intentions suggested for its model reader. Likewise, the model author is a strategy of the text, speaking to the reader as a narrator, either as a representation of the empirical author or as an impersonal construct permeating the text, addressing the reader in the third person or in the passive voice (the public opinion clams that…, it is decided that…). The model author is a textual strategy built-in into the text in order to guide the model reader to certain interpretations and away from others.

How does the text communicate with the reader? There are a number of ways of analysing this. Among them, a kind of rhetorical analysis, focusing on the classical tropes, is perhaps particularly popular among ethnographers. Irish philosopher Kenneth Burke (1945) lists the following four major tropes: metaphor, metonymy, synecdoche and irony. The ethnographer may wish to identify tropes and to find out how they help to communicate the text's messages from model author to model reader. Metaphor is an unusual usage of words in a new context so that they acquire new meaning, drawing attention to certain aspects of the topic. Metonymy is an expression where one word serves as a semantic representative of another word. Synecdoche is a kind of metonymy where the part represents the whole. Irony is a feature of a style in the text which implies a deliberate contradiction between the literary meaning of the utterance and its actual meaning that is not expressed directly, often provoking mirth or laughter. Quite often, an ironic style comes with a strong use of metaphors.

The tropes can be quite informative for ethnographers because they are connected with much more than just the communicative potential of a text. Swedish organization theorist Kaj Sköldberg (1990) connects the tropes to the poetic logic of organizations and communities. Different types of structures and leadership style are manifestations of poetic logics directed by leading communicative tropes. The dominating trope can tell us much about the organizational culture as a whole. Changes and transitions between different structural and value systems can also be followed and traced thanks to an analysis of the main classical four tropes used as part of their communication.

BOX 5.1   MEETING HISTORY, BY ANNA MODZELEWSKA

Inspired by organizational ethnography, I have, for six years, been conducting qualitative research focusing on the original organizational structures of the Independent Self-Governing Trade Union 'Solidarity' (NSZZ 'Solidarność'), as they were constructed in the 1980s. I conducted numerous in-depth interviews with former organizers and activists, I analysed existing materials, and engaged in observation, of course prospectively, as I could not make a journey into the past. In order to connect to the past, I analysed historical testimonies as part of my field material. Together, it made it pos-

sible to construct and reconstruct stories stretched over time and in order
to better understand the processes and their consequences. Organizational
historiographer Tomasz Ochinowski (2017) emphasizes that the role of the
researcher dealing with such material is not so much to describe, but rather
to understand, history.

Historical materials were the starting point for understanding the social
phenomena taking place nearly 40 years ago, and gave me the context in
which my research participants were active. Above all, they allowed me to
better prepare for interviews. Often, the interviewees provided me with materials, leaflets, notes, and drawings that were important to them during the
period of their activity in the movement, and which now constitute a testi-
mony of their activities. The leaflets were informative: they instructed how
to establish a union structure, how to proclaim a strike, and about the rules
that should be implemented during a protest. Some of them were examples
of actual organizational structures: representations of factory committees
were drawn. I also used to show them to my interviewees, to help them to
recreate the history from years past, to bring back reminiscences.

My historical knowledge also helped to gain trust from my interviewees.
They saw me as someone who understands the past better and started to
offer more personal stories, referring to their family histories, especially
the underground activity from the Second World War, which inspired them
to act the way they did in the 1980s. Here are examples of what two of my
interviewees said on the topic:

> We always refer to history. This is where it starts. Without history, there would
> be no 'Solidarity'. It is important to us. (Zbigniew Ferczyk, soldier of the Home
> Army, Kraków activist of Solidarity during martial law)
> After the introduction of martial law, Solidarity was an underground state […]. It
> was the third underground state of this kind [in Poland]. The first is the January
> Uprising [1863–1864]. The second the [Nazi] occupation. […] Of course, there
> was no army, no judiciary, and no courts of law. […But] there were governing
> bodies, and the press, the radio: media. (Bogdan Borusewicz, one of the main
> organizers of the strike at the Gdańsk Lenin Shipyard in August 1980)

As we can see, they were often referring back and forth between different
historical contexts, as ways of searching for an image of truth and probability. Research combining interviews with historical texts allowed me to better
understand the context of the phenomena I was studying, especially those
that cannot be observed in real time. This is triangulation at work: a comprehensive perspective emerging from, on the one hand, the subjective tes-
timony of the respondents, and on the other hand, the written testimonies
of the bygone past.

Finally, there is the large question – or, indeed, many questions, of context. The example in Box 5.1 shows how the knowledge of history informs the picture of the studied field as well as connects to further layers of contextual meaning. Umberto Eco (1990) claims that finding the intentions of the text is only possible by comparing fragments with the whole, by contextual analysis, characteristic for ethnographic methods. But it should also be compared against the larger context in which it has been written. One of the less appealing tendencies in much contemporary reading of texts is the tendency to read them ahistorically and anachronistically, in disregard of the historical context, and quite often with a sense of moral superiority. The contemporary reader and author, rarely engaging with texts older than 2–3 years, sometimes do read something from a more distant past, but quite often to judge them or to misread them, catching words and expressions that meant something else then compared with if they were spoken now. This is an unfortunately common pattern, stemming, most likely, from the recent depreciation of humanities in current education and an unreflexive use of quantitative methods (Zyphur et al. 2016). As the example in Box 5.1 shows, it is vital to apply a historical sensibility in order to achieve a contextualization that can be quite illuminating not just for the reading of a text but for the entire study. Polish organization theorist Tomasz Ochinowski (2017) advises using a historiographic method in the reading of texts written in the past and to triangulate the interpretations with other sources, at least two others, published in other media. Or, as Anna Modzelewska's example shows, by both reading historical materials and interviewing social actors who had been participating in social life in the past (of course providing that these can be found). Tomasz Ochinowski presents this method as one which enables creating a reflexive, contexualized organizational memory, a framework for research based on 'historical thinking' (Ochinowski 2017: 41).

Another useful method for a achieving a wider contextualization is cultural analysis. In the words of American sociologist Norman Denzin, its aim is to capture and understand workings of the text that are 'unconscious, unintentional' by directing attention 'to the problem of how the history that human beings make and live spontaneously is determined by structures of meaning that they have not chosen for themselves' (Denzin 1992: 74). The researcher looks for traces of ideological and strategic messages and brings them forward, explaining what the text 'does' to the reader. Such readings are explicitly critical:

> Such textual readings attempt to show how specific texts create their particular images of subjects and their experiences. These readings attempt to examine the narrative-writing strategies that structure the texts' treatment of text and author, presence and lived experience, the real and its representations, and the subject and intentionality. (Denzin 1992: 82)

The aim of cultural analysis of this kind is to better understand not just the text itself but its intended readers. It is a good idea to talk about one's interpretations of texts with interviewees from the field, as Anna Modzelewska has done, since they are the people who are 'naturally suited' to be the recipients of the text.

5.2   STORIES AND THICK DESCRIPTION

There are many uses of stories in ethnographic research. It can be said that ethnography is all about the collecting and processing of stories, and presenting the results in the form of yet more stories, with literary qualities of their own (Clifford and Marcus 1986). The main such quality that, at the same time, both reflects and defines much of what ethnographic method is about, is known as thick description (Geertz 1973).

BOX 5.2   POETIC JOURNEY, BY JOANNA ŚREDNICKA

I conducted a longitudinal and immersive ethnographic study of a Polish organization: a part of an international corporation in the ceramics industry. I entered, then left, and then returned to the field many times, with the most intense phase of my frequent presence lasting for two years. I was involved in various fieldwork activities, including open interviews, simulation game-based workshops, and direct and participant observations during various company events. My research aimed at an understanding of the mechanisms behind collaboration, and in particular of the identification processes underlying cooperative behaviours.

The more time I spent in the field, the more my thoughts and interpretations started revolving around cultural themes which I recognized from romantic nineteenth-century poetry. Following the recommendations of Clifford Geertz to explore the wider cultural context I delved into romantic poetry, which turned out to be extremely helpful in exploring the identity formation processes. Then I came across an interesting phenomenon; well-known to someone versed in romantic poetry, but surprising in the context of business. I called it the 'micro-romantic uprisings' of managers who engaged in resistance despite top management's rulings, the undertaking of guerrilla activities. Here are some examples of my notes from the field from that time.

> It is my third visit to the factory. The director was very talkative and direct today. Most of the time, we were talking about corporation; again. From our previous conversations I know that he is very committed to his work. I was quite sur-

prised when he suddenly revealed his current strategy of dealing with malicious corporate strategies. 'I am just doing things sometimes secretly or hiding some data because the corporation shouldn't know it. This is sometimes the only way to make things you believe are important and necessary.' When he said these words, I knew that I had heard them somewhere, that it was a recurring theme. Few weeks before Michał, the director of product development, shared with me a very similar story. He was emotional and dedicated. We met in a cafe. Michał talked about his bold idea of changing the corporation from inside, without looking back, by doing his job the best he can. He seemed desperate and quite optimistic. 'My model is simple: doing everything you can, without looking at any procedures and corporate rules. If the president of the corporation saw what I do every day, he would take an axe to my head.'

My journey to the world of poetry helped me to grasp the complexity of the social reality, but what I value even more, was to be able to understand how values such as the ones expressed in the poem below (by Wincenty Pol, nineteenth-century Polish romantic; translation by Jonas-Dębska) were constantly inspiring the identity formation processes:

> From free-born tree
> The leaves are flown;
> By the grave, a bird
> Sings alone.
> No hope for Poland
> To be saved!
> The dream is done,
> your sons in the grave.
> The villages burnt,
> The towns laid low,
> A woman in the field
> Sings of her woe.
> Now all are gone,
> Taken their scythes;
> None now to work,
> The harvest dies....
> The battle's over,
> But nothing's done,
> To the fields the men
> Do not return.
> Some lying in earth,
> Or prisoners made;
> Some lost their homes,
> Afar have strayed.
> No help from heaven
> Or human hand.
> Blossoms in vain
> The wasted land.

Thanks to poetry, I was able to detect a sudden shift in cultural themes reflected in organizational narratives. One such fundamental shift, from the bravery of 'micro-romantic uprisings' to a sense of hopelessness that followed, was particularly illuminating.

> The second time we meet in a cafe. Michał is visibly moved. He often uses the words *values* and *principles*. He uses gestures, raises his voice, and lowers it conspiratorially a few times. A completely different conversation than we had had just a few months before when he was full of bravery and quite optimistic. Now the corporation has been taken over by an investment fund, and Michał sees how this is a threat to everything that is locally important. He presents it as the embodiment of short-sightedness and the pursuit of quick profits at the expense of local interests and reasonable long-term development. His words are filled with melancholy, a feeling of loss, the conviction that 'what's good is behind us'. He speaks of the disappointment in managers who prefer immediate benefits over long-term development. This time Michał doesn't talk about any bold ideas of changing the corporation from inside, without looking back, by doing his job the best he can. Today he seems hopeless. 'No help from heaven' *I lost hope; it seems to me that all this idea, all this strategy, that we're going to send our people to the corporation to change that corporation, is failing now. It seems to me that corporation cannot be changed, not in that way.*

Box 5.2 shows the sensitivity of Joanna Średnicka towards emerging stories in her field and in the writing up of her results. Also, the need for such stories made her focus on certain plots more than on others. She was following in the footsteps of classic American anthropologist Clifford Geertz, who advised looking for and actively using description that contains rich content and a multitude of potential interpretations; neither normatively nor functionally taken out of context. Geertz's *thick description* has the ability to create a sense of participation by the reader in the real life of the protagonists. It is not just a simple report of what had happened but presented in such a way as to enable multiple and personal readings, resonating on the intellectual as well as sensual and emotional levels. Giving an example of a Balinese cockfight from his own material, he proposes that elements and objects that do not fulfil any straightforward informative role, nonetheless are an important component of the ethnographic story: they facilitate an understanding of the facts in relationship to the context. Thick description facilitates an understanding of the 'normalness [of human beings] without reducing [their] particularity' (Geertz 1973: 14).

Joanna Średnicka took great care to perceive and to recreate the moods and affects of her field. The ethnographic genre is known for its narrative concern. American organization theorist John Van Maanen presents the most characteristic styles of writing ethnography in his celebrated book, *Tales of the Field* (1988): realist tales, confessional tales and impressionist tales. The classical mode of writing ethnography is the realist convention; a story devoid of emotions, written in the third person and striving at faithfulness and reliability of the account, yet depicting the 'comings and goings of members of the culture' (Van Maanen 1988: 45) with an ambition to achieve authenticity of representation. Confessional tales are highly personalized, describing the feelings of the author, including sensual impressions, doubts and dilemmas. The narrator is constructed as a character that has experienced the described events and can therefore vouch for their truthfulness and authenticity. Impressionist tales are consciously created in a literary form, aimed at making an impression on the readers and getting them involved in the depicted scenes and events. They use 'words, metaphors, phrasings, imagery, and most critically, the expansive recall of fieldwork experience' (Van Maanen 1988: 102). This is a demanding style of writing and, at best, it is able to attract broader readership than just the standard academic audience, giving a sense of sharing the experience, engaging readers as if they had been in the field themselves.

All these styles can be combined in ethnographic writings, as they usually are in the material ethnographers collect in the field, through interviews or in texts from the field. There are many other possible styles, among them critical tales of political engagement or jointly-told tales, co-authored within the field or by research participants and researchers. The main point is to be aware of and honest about the style of the stories one collects in, as well as authors about, the field (Van Maanen 1995). The matter of style should also be consciously considered while preparing fieldnotes. The ways they are taken and organized enables or makes difficult further stylistic uses. It is a good idea to take notes in a way including evocation of sensory detail, images and scenes, and stories angled from different perspectives, such as moods and snippets of conversations (Emerson et al., 2011). The writing of fieldnotes is part of a larger interactive and interpretive process and it is important to keep it in mind and use it to its full potential.

5.3   DEEPER NARRATIVES

Stories, also those mundane everyday tales collected in the field, are about more than meets the eye. Organization theorists and philosophers Hugo Letiche and Jean-Luc Moriceau (2019) point to the sense-making layer in communications and texts that demand an aesthetic approach to be seen and understood. They speak of the art of making sense which involves the senses but also human sensibilities and sensitivities. The art of sense-making is connected with perception and construction, as well as with the experience of beauty. It is not purely intellectual but embodied and based on judgement not only reflection and thinking. It is vital to use expressions that allow for a plurality of senses, not limiting understanding to just one way of making sense. Fairly linear narratives are not enough to embrace these deeper aesthetic dimensions. Artistic methods, open to the symbolic, expressive and affective in communication are necessary to include them.[1] There are a number of possible artistic approaches to ethnographic field material, of which we would like to recommend three which we consider particularly useful: a focus on myths, archetypes and fairy tales.

BOX 5.3   THE MYSTERY OF CREATIVITY, BY MONIKA BROSZKIEWICZ, MARTYNA MAJKA AND JULIA PODLEWSKA

Fascinating and mysterious worlds of art and creation... What is the creative process? We convinced a few artists to allow us to study them at work and we set out to explore these big questions by arts-based methods and interview. We supplemented our research work with presentations and films related to the subject.

First we observed each of the artists, trying to see how and wherefrom they got their inspiration, and how they were preparing the creative progress. Then we observed them at work and its effects. We took photos during the whole process. We finally made a short film: our reflection of the process itself and the photographs we took. We are enjoying the film and how it, by itself, is a creative product.

Initially, we were not involved in the creative process, but were non-participant observers of such processes. We conducted the research separately. We did not interact with each other in any way during the initial stages of the process itself. We wanted to stay as invisible as possible, and not to influence the field. We did, however, cause some confusion at the beginning, and we felt insecure, too. However, over time, when the artists focused more and more on their work, everyone fell into their rhythms. Thanks to this, we were able to look closely at the behaviour of each of the artists and also gained a creative experience of our own. We tried to capture the emotions, the affects, and of course the behaviour of people involved in the project.

All the artists expressed the idea that art influences their lives very strongly. Each of them also thought of their future in connection with art. Nobody was able to count how much time they devote to creative work, but in our observation we had the impression that it was a great deal, certainly not less than the standard working day. But all of it was not about 'production', even something recognizable as activity. Much of the time they engaged in thinking, doing preparatory work and some refining or cleaning up the actual work. One exception turned out to be a musician who did not do much preparation. All the interviewees were quite focused on their emotions except the cinematographer, who could not only be inspired by his own creative impulse, but must take into account the director's suggestions. But quite many of them interacted a lot with others or were thinking of other people during their creative process. As, in fact, did we.

The example in Box 5.3 is a multi-layered study, containing ethnographic and creative elements, on the part of the research participants as well as of the researchers. Who is doing creative work and what does it mean? Are artists creative only when they 'produce'? Are ethnographers creative as well and what sense? These questions mix and intertwine in the story by Monika Broszkiewicz, Martyna Majka and Julia Podlewska and it is perhaps their entanglement that makes the story interesting. To study the creative field in order to find out that one is creative oneself is not a simple narrative but one that aims a bit deeper. One observed reality was the behavioural and communicational. But there was one underneath it, consisting of emotions, affects and of the idea of creation and creativity itself.

According to Joseph Campbell (1988), myths connect two realities: the external, everything we experience as 'the outside', 'the reality'; and the internal, what we feel is 'in the mind' or the matter of our inner life. The former provides images and symbols, including language and a cultural frame that makes it possible to communicate with others. The latter offers awareness and a sense of being the experiencing subject, learning, thinking and feeling. The connection happens by metaphors and should not be taken literally. A literal reading of myths is usually a more or less gross misreading. We agree with Yiannis Gabriel (2004) that myth is a powerful tool for understanding contemporary organizations on deeper levels. Using myth to explore organizations has become both alluring and respectable, especially among organizational ethnographers. However, Gabriel warns against a banalization of myth: it should apply to all kinds of narratives, not only to those that touch upon the sphere of the spiritual, sacred or transcendent. But myths may throw a light on the sphere of the profane, providing characters, themes, and metaphors. They help people cope with existential questions, such as life, death, love, friendship, betrayal, etc.

Some stories are particularly powerful because they resonate with some deep recurrent patterns in human culture, known as archetypes. According to Carl Gustav Jung (1981 [1934]), the Swiss psychiatrist who developed the idea of psychological relevance of the archetypes, they are empty slots, like riverbeds in the collective unconscious, ready to hold images, symbols, and narrative plots. The archetypes come up in myths and art as strong characters: gods and goddesses, kings and queens, love and adventure, as well as in folk tales and popular songs. Archetypes as such are neither good nor bad; they all have both a light and a dark side. More mundane tales, such as stories from the field, may also contain archetypes as characters, plots or settings. Such archetypical tales tend to serve as particularly important clues for sense-making in the studied community or organization (Kostera 2012). Both the important absences and the significant presences in organizations can be best understood with the help of archetypes such as the king, the sage and the trickster. They hold massive significance for organizational cultures, and a potential for renewal, but, if they are not engaged with consciously, they may have a deleterious effect on a community and its participants. Finally, legends, fairy tales and fantastic stories can also serve to understand what is happening in the field on a deeper level. Organization theorist Anna Zueva (2021) explains that a deep connection to themes and characters present in fairy tales can help the ethnographer in making sense of the liminal, ambivalent and multifaceted in ways that allow her to retain the complexity and yet steer clear of conceptual chaos. As Zueva points out, the ethnographer must dismantle stereotypes and recognize that our understanding is never final – and fairy tales as methodological metaphors help with both.

The example in Box 5.4 shows how myths and field research sometimes merge and intertwine, Arkadiusz Kłos and Ewa Kruk were experienced managers at the time they enrolled a course in organizational ethnography. They wished to study something quite unlike their everyday reality, something truly magical. And who of us, viewers of Wim Wenders' sublime *Wings of Desire* (1987), readers of novels by Isaac Bashevis Singer featuring acrobats, admirers of Marc Chagall's magnificent grand circus, can consider themselves immune from that magic? And who, as a kid, never ever dreamed of running away with the circus?

BOX 5.4   RESEARCHING ENCHANTMENT, BY ARKADIUSZ KŁOS AND EWA KRUK

In 2009/2010 we carried out a study focused on management methods adopted in the creative industries. We focused on a Polish travelling circus, using participant observation, non-participant observation, open-ended interview and historical data gathering. Our ethnography was as a multidimensional journey. A journey through space, because during this season circus travelled 7,500 km, giving performances in 183 places. A journey back in time through centuries of circus history and traditions. And, most importantly, a journey within the organization itself as well as a journey within ourselves: observers, ethnographers... To feel the atmosphere of a place where nomadic movement is part of everyday life we travelled hundreds kilometres with the circus.

At our first visit the red canopy of the big circus tent, placed between grey buildings and a row of garages, seemed to us an exotic island emerging in a grey reality. Charming, so similar to old Gypsy caravans lined up in a circle, inside which a colourful and noisy village flourished every evening. We admired the nomadic mentality of people, moving with extreme lightness, spending many months in their vehicles which became their home. Mobile and yet perfectly organized people, separated from their families for many months of the year. Their motto was: 'you don't work in a circus – you live the circus'. It fascinated and entertained us to immerse ourselves in the culture of organization, so different from our static daily work and lifestyle.

Curiosity was, from the beginning, a strong motivation for in-depth research. We concentrated on the people and the interactions between them. When onstage, during the two-hour show, in the glare of the spotlights and in sequin costumes, their life seemed magical and surreal. But when the lights went out, the circus turned out to be a place of hard work and sacrifice. Both modes attracted our curiosity.

Our research lasted for about nine months, which is the length of an average circus season. Relationships with our interlocutors changed over time. Our conversations became deep and sincere. They let us look behind the circus front that few people can pass behind. Each subsequent interview changed our perception of the entire group. Our research participants came from many countries, creating a colourful mix of cultures and personalities. They opened up to us, enabling us to make a specific journey into the depths of people, a journey more exotic the more their lives were different from ours. Of course, we did not collect pure empirical data devoid of subjectivity. The studied reality and our perception fused and merged, and changed each other.

Our circus ethnography awakened many emotions and left a permanent mark on us. The enchantment of the circus, but also getting to know and to understand a culture of hard work and organization showed us that we, too, can work differently, manage differently, live differently. The study initiated changes that are still happening. Some subtle and some very important, such as changing the workplace. Some huge. The open-mindedness of observers that accompanies us every day.

Arkadiusz Kłos and Ewa Kruk also took some beautiful pictures of their fieldwork in both its main modes: the enchantment of the performance and the everyday hard work. These images invoke all the fairy tales and mythical narratives familiar to people grown up in European culture. And they also create an ethnographic conversation, their own, between the magical and the mundane.

5.4   ROLE AND DRAMA

People in the field play a variety of social roles. In order to focus on how this happens, a theatrical lens can be applied as a methodological metaphor for reading material from the field, and as the genre of writing up parts of the study. Canadian sociologist Erving Goffman dedicated much of his work to show how people play roles with the aim of influencing others. He argues that they first and foremost do so in order to make a connection, to engage with others (Goffman 1959). In order to make a community or an organization work, everyone does not have to agree about everything, or be completely clear about one's motives. As in theatre, the motifs of the characters may be hidden, and it is sufficient to know whose cue is when and what response is to be expected. Nonetheless, the drama consists of both what is said, what is left unsaid and how it happens. A model useful for analysing drama as well as ethnographic material from this complex perspective is known as Burke's pentad (1945) and consists of five elements. In the words of the author himself:

> They are: Act, Scene, Agent, Agency, Purpose. In a rounded statement about motives, you must have some word that names the act (names what took place, in thought or deed), and another that names the scene (the background of the act, the situation in which it occurred); also, you must indicate what person or kind of person (agent) performed the act, what means or instruments he used (agency), and the purpose. Men may violently disagree about the purposes behind a given act, or about the character of the person who did it, or how he did it, or in what kind of situation he acted; or they may even insist upon totally different words to name the act itself. But be that as it may, any complete statement about motives will offer some kind of answers to these five questions: what was done (act), when or where it was done (scene), who did it (agent), how he did it (agency), and why (purpose) (Burke 1945: 15)

Social scientists Iain Mangham and Michael Overington (1987) use the pentad to depict contemporary organizations. As presented in the book *Organizations as Theatre*, they both observe and interpret their field through this epistemological lens. They sit in management meetings, take notes as if they were cues in drama and present what they see in the form of a theatrical play. What becomes visible is the social, the relational, and, of course, the conversational. They present the scenery, gestures, statements of the participants and reactions that they evoke, and show that all this not only creates the atmosphere of the event, but the very content of the meeting. For them, theatre gives an opportunity to consider the meanings of apparently shallow or mundane gestures, it 'creates space for awareness' (Mangham and Overington 1987: 101). It can be brought forward only when the observer is himself aware of the theatricality of social performance and its deeper cultural and social layers.

The dramatic character of the social makes culture potentially creative and open to interpretations and re-interpretations. It can also be used as a cynical and manipulative management strategy, as in American sociologist Arlie Hochschild's (1983) depiction of professions such as flight attendants, nurses and waiters, where the acting out of emotions is an important element. In contemporary service organizations, emotions are often managed in a way that leads to commercial gain by providing 'customer satisfaction' at the cost of alienation of the workers. Social actors that perform such roles often suppress their real feelings, tending in the longer run to burnout and loss of touch with emotions or with the professional role.

BOX 5.5 STAGING NORMALITY, BY KINGA CZOWICKA, DOMINIKA DĘBOWSKA, JOANNA SIWEK AND ZOFIA SULIKOWSKA

It seems like a world we know, yet it is not. Seven months have passed since the second lockdown. On Saturday 15 May 2021, the government allowed for the lifting of some of the restrictions introduced during the pandemic of Covid-19: it is no longer necessary to wear masks outdoors, and food gardens can open. For the first time in over half a year's time people can actually meet in their favourite cafe.

And here we were again, strolling around the square's tarmac, tasting coffee from a popular chain, sitting in the café's garden. No one knew we were observers; we looked pretty much like all those who decided to go out that day and take advantage of the new-old circumstances. You could meet people representing every age group, whether individually or in a group.

But at a first glance, one can see that the predominant social participants on this day are families with children and older people. From the sidelines, everything may seem as it used to. But through direct observation of reality that we were able to understand the deeper mood of the day – by focusing on how people were playing their 'normal' roles.

There are many guests in each restaurant. It does not help that some of the tables were out of use. Customers do not really care about keeping the distance in the queues for their order or on their way to the toilet, and although everyone has a mask, it is rarely worn in the correct way. The casualness that can be seen at first glance is at odds with the atmosphere of mutual observation. People are observing each other and as if adapting as they go along. This creates a sense that something is not quite as it should be. Out of the ordinary. Everyone seems to be intensely interested in what is going on around them, and less focused on their phone, which tends to be the standard time-killer in such situations. It feels as if everyone is extra watchful and somehow trying extra hard to play their old roles 'as if everything was normal'. And there is also the constant presence of a police patrol, circling the Main Square eight times within three hours.

We sit down at the only free table, even though it is not disinfected. No one points out to us that the table is not available yet. The staff have their hands full that day, it's hard for them to disinfect and clean regularly while giving and serving orders. We decide to ask the busy waitress to disinfect. However, we still have to wait an extra 10 minutes for the table to be cleared. There are not enough personnel to deal with the crowds, which is fairly normal for a chain café but even so – excessive.

On the one hand, there is a sense of people enjoying the long-awaited freedom and showing a gentle lack of concern with the general rules of precaution in public places. On the other hand, we also catch an aura of overwhelming uncertainty, maybe due to the tell-tale police presence. Sanitary rules have become firmly established for some customers: some mothers admonish their children to disinfect their hands before eating. We listen to conversations. Vaccinations seem to be among the dominant topics in the bustle of chat; more than the weather. Health care seems to have become a classic small talk topic.

The real surprise, however, awaits us in one of the most popular places in Kraków in recent times – Hala Forum, a complex of restaurants and bars located in the building of the old, no longer operational, Hotel Forum. The regulations issued by the government clearly decree that only outdoors gastronomic establishments would be allowed to open. However, due to the weather, which shifted from sunny to rainy, the party moved indoors. We do not see anyone sitting on specially prepared deckchairs, the pandemic-time scene ready for the guests. But it is all empty. None of us had seen so many people in one place, not for a long time. It is a strange feeling, not only to see so many people, but also to see so many people without masks, indoors. We unanimously agree that the door to the Forum Hall was a bit like a portal that took us back to the time before the pandemic. Being inside the former hotel, one could really feel that way; there was a play carefully staged. It was a very nice feeling to some degree: many longed for 'normality' and what was before the pandemic. On the other hand, however, small gestures, the watchfulness, a certain tension revealed an undercurrent of uncertainty. The desire to socialize and meet friends in the city after a long time for everyone present on that day in the Forum Hall seem irresistible and the 'normal' social roles are being played with extra insistence.

Our observation became the basis for creating an ethnographic pandemic game, the scenario of which depends on the answers given in real time. The protagonists, deciding to meet virtually, find out that one of us – Dominika

– is stuck in an alternative world of the intertwined past and present. One by one, the evidence she represents in the form of photographs and films testifies to her imprisonment and the absolute dependence of her fate on the decisions of the others. The link with the virtual game for Dominika's life ends up in the hands of the other girls who, acting under the pressure of time and supernatural manipulations of events, try to bring her back to the here and now. The stakes are not unique and do not concern Dominika alone – wrong decisions by the others will cause all the players' characters to be erased from the future.

Organization theorists Heather Höpfl and Steve Linstead (1993) argue that the managed performance usually tries to hide the ambiguities that are inherent in theatre and constitutes the basis of artistic expression. If feelings do not fit into a managed performance, they are eliminated. Social actors cannot use all the range of their emotions and experiences to offer a more original interpretation of their roles. If management had more of a dramatic consciousness and were respectful towards theatrical dimensions of social interaction, the creative potential of everyday life would be much greater, as it has an artistic dimension. And so does field research in even the most mundane social settings. In Box 5.5, Kinga Czowicka, Dominika Dębowska, Joanna Siwek, and Zofia Sulikowska observed urban scenes as if they were performances, staged to enact urban life from before the pandemic. Social actors behaved as if time had gone back to before the lockdowns of 2020. They decided they would present their material in the form of short dramatic episodes, unravelling as in a role playing game, when the choice of response triggers a specific scene.

NOTE

1. The book edited by Jean-Luc Moriceau, Hugo Letiche and Marie-Astrid Le Theule (2019) offers a comprehensive epistemological and philosophical frame for such an approach to research and interpretation in social studies.

6. Good ethnographic research?

6.1 METHODOLOGICAL PRINCIPLES

There are very few strict rules how to do ethnography, but there are several important principles that ethnographers all over the world uphold and cherish (see for example Pachirat 2018). The most important of them we have already addressed elsewhere: the imperative of engaged and prolonged presence, requiring the building of relationships based on trust (see Chapter 3) and the contextualized approach to research and reporting, known as thick description (see Chapter 5). One can say that all the other principles derive from these two, including matters of ethics and the emergence of patterns, on which we will elaborate in this chapter. We suggest that the reader keeps that in mind; we will from time to time refer to these fundamental issues in order to show how the system of ethnographer's principles hangs together.

BOX 6.1   PRINCIPLES, BY ADRIANNA BRZUSKA,
IZABELA KURZYK AND PAWEŁ
MICHALCZUK

Poland, 2021, the Covid-19 pandemic. Everyone's lives were changed, remain changed. Isolation has led to a re-evaluation of priorities, it affected bodies, psyches and relationships. We wished to explore some of the first waves of these changes in our ethnographically inspired project. Our first observations began in neutral and everyday places: a popular major shopping centre, people commuting to work (again), people going to the cinema, riding the tram. On the face of it, each of these everyday activities seems not to be connected to anything much, but, ethnographic observation makes the observer sensitive and attentive. We saw a connecting link between these everyday situations. Affect. Fear, uncertainty, anxiety, hope, excitement. Despite the masks, we could read these in the eyes of the people we were observing.

But was it ethnographic enough to just stare, to imagine that we know what people are feeling? And were we really attentive enough to the others' emotions? We felt we needed to talk with other people, and decided to conduct some open-ended interviews. We thought about whom to talk with in the short time that was assigned to our fieldwork and thought it would be sensible to interview people most likely to open up to us: our friends. The igniting moment would be the creation of a unique artwork. They created poems and images and we proceeded to talk with that work of art as a starting point.

It was very important to us that the interviews took place live and face-to-face. Our questions elicited responses that were often quite surprising to us. We felt the interviewees made extra effort to be honest and to share their feelings with us. They all explained how the pandemic has blocked them emotionally, and how each of them, with a different life baggage, different temperament, felt somehow externalized in their own lives. And they were willing to talk with us about it.

Thanks to the interviews, we began to understand the emotions we were observing better and we no longer felt we were trespassing on others' affects, no longer like we were outsiders staring at others. Maybe this change was due to the fact that our interviewees began their conversations with us each with their own work of art. None of them was a professional artist but each created something of their own, and igniting that spark of creativity inside them produced an equally sensitive and creative spark in each of us, too. Now we felt we were better equipped to investigate ethnographically the strange and yet familiar everyday reality we are all immersed in.

Our project, entitled 'New/old reality: talking about a pandemic' evoked some conversations, some conclusions and many emotions in us as researchers, in the interlocutors as well as in our audience when we presented it.

The authors (Box 6.1) of a short project about people's everyday reality during the pandemic were particularly concerned about confidence and sincerity. They opted for face-to-face interviews, with appropriate safety measures, in order to create a bond with the interviewees that would be conducive to honesty and the sharing of feelings. They asked their interlocutors for artistic expressions of their emotions, such as poems and visual art, which they presented in the form of an online exhibition.[1] The imperative of engagement and thick description led the authors to a deep reflexivity during the research project and its presentation. Personal artistic resonance is the basis for their knowledge claim, and intensive engagement with the interviewees forms the basis for the trustworthiness of their study.

Professors of education Yvonne Lincoln and Egon Guba (1985) purport that trustworthiness is the main criterion for good qualitative research and it means using credible methods, and the possibility of relating the results to similar objects and situations. Credibility is about reliability of the research process and it can be improved by triangulation, that is, the use of more than one research method. In ethnographic research, triangulation is an imperative. It improves credibility and it also provides good material for reflexivity. The ethnographer should also take care to provide an account of her activities in the field. There is no need to strive for replicability in qualitative research, in fact that would be plainly impossible, but it is more crucial to detail what and how it has been done in order to provide the presented material. It is particularly important to provide a detailed account for all the omissions, mistakes, misunderstandings and possible blindspots. This can improve the usefulness of the study results for other researchers, as it can make it easier for them to apply and adapt the conclusions to their own areas of interest. The results of an ethnography concern processes, and if a detailed account of how these processes were studied is provided, the risk of blackboxing or repeating, and even magnifying, errors and misunderstandings is lowered. Ethnographic research should be useful to more than the immediate participants of research. The researcher should be able to understand how, and in what way, the research can be used in varying contexts. Trustworthiness of ethnographic research also means that readers from other contexts can rely on some aspects of the conclusions, especially these pertaining to the social and cultural dynamics of the studied phenomena. For example, we may not all have experienced exactly the same emotions as the protagonists of the study presented in Box 6.1 during the lockdown, and we may not have produced similar artwork, but we may all recognize some of the reactions and empathize with the protagonists, especially if we understand how the authors of the study communicated with them and what is the supposed role of the art.

The positivist rules of objectivity and avoidance of researcher bias do not apply to ethnography, which is idiographic and inductive/abductive, rather than deductive. This means that no hypotheses are constructed beforehand but the material from the research leads the process of theory formulation. Inductive research should ideally be entirely based on empirical patterns with no prior assumptions at all on the part of the researcher. In practice, most of ethnographic work is abductive, i.e. some reasonable assumptions and framing take place during the research (Czarniawska 2014). The principles of research design for trustworthiness in ethnographic fieldwork differ quite firmly from positivist ones. Peregrine Schwartz-Shea and Dvora Yanow (2012) outline some of the key ways of strengthening the quality of interpretive research by the continuous checking of researcher sense-making – a way of making sure that the abductive or inductive processes lead to trustworthy knowledge claims. First, the research should be reflexive, that is the researcher should 'pursue an active consideration of engagement with the ways in which his own sense-making and the particular circumstances that might have affected it, throughout all phase of the research process, relate to the knowledge claims he ultimately advances in written form' (Schwartz-Shea and Yanow 2012: 100). For example, the study presented in Box 6.1 constantly engaged in a reflection of how the researcher's own presence affected the interactions, as well as the identities of all the participants. Second, a check of the researcher's sense-making during data generation and analysis is needed. The aim is not to 'get the facts right' as in positivist research but, rather, to make sure that different viewpoints are well represented. The authors of the project in Box 6.1 encouraged such different readings during an online 'vernissage' of the artwork created by the interviewees where the authors also presented their interpretations. Ethnographers should strive for transparency in their reflexive checks, involving different audiences and perspectives.

Trustworthiness is also improved by authentic material derived from the field, not just in the form of the researcher's notes and stories, but from citations from interviews, bringing real voices from the field. A spirit of sensible cultural relativism, observing and respecting the diversity and distinctness of both societies and individuals is to be recommended (Clifford and Marcus 1986), perhaps without any extreme attempts at 'going native' or completely adopting the mindframes of the field, because that causes a lack of reflexivity that is deleterious to the trustworthiness of ethnographic texts.

Ethnographies should have a temporal authority, that is, be grounded in relatively long-lasting studies, which both strengthens the authority of the material, based on personal experiential immersion, and enables discerning interesting patterns of culture (Pachirat 2018). The central issue of contribution to knowledge concerns, in the case of ethnographic studies, typically processes and dynamics (more of which in the final section of this chapter). But it may also throw light on other aspects of human experience and condition. These need to be explicitly stated, for example in the conclusions. Therefore, the need to account not just for one's own doings but also feelings may be of importance: how were these (but not other) experiences observed and why do they matter to the researcher and why, eventually, should the reader care.

In summary, good ethnographic research should provide something new to our knowledge. It can be a new phenomenon or a phenomenon we already know, albeit in different contexts, or reveal less known connections between its internal elements. Deeper connections are what we usually look for in ethnographic research, layers of meaning beneath the better known and more superficial levels of knowing. A good rule of thumb is to check first if what we intend to study can be measured and counted. If it can, then, most probably, quantitative methods should be adopted to study it. If not, then qualitative methods may be more suitable. If a hypothesis can be formulated, then one should do a quantitative study. If not and we do not know what will emerge from the study – and that is the whole point of it – then ethnography may be the way to go. If the researcher cannot think about any simple questions that can be asked in a survey, then she should consider ethnographic methods.

6.2   ETHICAL PRINCIPLES

It has nowadays become standard practice in academia to consider ethnical issues in research as if all of it were based on positivist principles and mostly carried out in laboratories. Swedish sociologist David Wästerfors (2019) argues that this has serious and deleterious consequences for ethnographic research where the very principles demand different sensibilities and criteria of ethical judgement, and the current praxis disregards real moral dilemma and imposes unnecessary rigours that make ethnographic research close to impossible. The contemporary ethical regulations that are applied in many countries, and in particular at Anglo-Saxon universities, make it obligatory to pass ethnical approval after review by an ethical committee. The committees usually presuppose research based on a definite sample, with a clear and unchangeable problem and hypotheses to be tested, and predictable procedures applied to subjects with whom the researcher has no closer relation. None of these assumptions is correct for ethnographic research. Guessing what the research will bring is either mendacious or harmful in ethnographic studies, and manipulating who and who not would participate in research is damaging for the study's trustworthiness. Furthermore, explicit consent is demanded from participants, usually signed on paper. It is difficult or even impossible to acquire such consent in the case of non-participant observation and on all ethnographic research situations it is irrelevant. The researcher does not study particular individuals but social processes and naturalistic contexts. Revealing the theme of the research is often quite destructive for the success of the research project which presupposes lack of 'contamination' and a naturalistic approach (Lincoln and Guba 1985). Furthermore, some research participants are wary of written, formal statements to sign. Yet a relationship of trust could be established with them by the researcher informally. One of us studied anarchist squats at some point and getting a signed statement from the organizers was practically impossible. It was a matter of choice: either to accept that and continue the research or pack up and leave the field.

David Wästerfors (2019) points out that a complex and living context where people talk and exchange experiences has to be summarized and crammed into a form. The formulas for accounting for what is regarded as correct in managerial terms is sharply at odds with ethnographic realities. Ethnography is about coming close to a community of people and trying to understand them – not about gaining control over them. Quite the opposite – a good ethnographer should not be in control of the researched situation. And yet the forms both assume that this is what takes place and forces the researcher to account for her work from such a perspective. At best this is a waste of time. There is no proof, Wästerfors points out, that this kind of humanistic research should have harmful effects for the studied communities, so it is in many cases just another useless bureaucratic exercise. However, much worse, it prevents the moral sensitivity that is needed in ethnographic research and forces the researcher to tell untruths or to resign from this methodology altogether. There are many anecdotal stories circulating in academic communities of how ethnography nowadays tends to get replaced either by autoethnography (which focuses on the researcher himself and his feelings) or case study (which is much easier to account for in ethical approval forms). In countries where it is possible to do ethnographic research without formalized ethical approval as long as no external funding is needed, ethnographers may not seek grants for this reason and leave the funding to quantitative colleagues. It makes their work easier but creates further disproportions in the already very unequal academic world.

BOX 6.2 AN ETHNOGRAPHY OF 'MY PEOPLE', BY KAROLINA WALATEK

The subject of my study was the protection of the local culture of a public school and its relationships with other organizations. The school was, yet again, facing the threat of liquidation. I was an ethnographer but also an ex-native myself, an ex-student and a person with roots in the local community. Over the course of a year, I conducted dozens of interviews with school staff, I engaged in observation and studied a large number of historical texts produced by the school. I also carried out some participant observations.

The school I investigated was located in a small town. In such a place there is a considerable emphasis on the locality of employees and associates: everybody knows everybody else and their parents and grandparents. An outsider would probably have been resisted, even rejected. However, as a kind of an insider I was facing many expectations to represent them well, to be faithful to 'my people'. I interviewed many staff members, I was immediately given access to the archives and I was allowed to enter the various events organized by the school.

The design of research methods was not just my choice, but also sprang from the necessity to adapt to the specifics of my field. I did not have the advantage of anonymity, and participant observation was only natural given the expectations directed at me to be there and to help out. The interviews by their nature were more like a friendly conversation than a formal contact. Anything else would have been awkward. During the duration of my study research I adapted to the schedule of my interviewees, usually meeting at school during breaks or other free time. The freedom to collect information was a considerable luxury. This is why my interviews varied in length (from three minutes to an hour) and the invitations to participate in events were spontaneous.

The 'open door' situation, which for many researchers would be a dream come true, presented me with new challenges, many of them of an ethical kind. While collecting materials and writing the empirical part, I had to face my own lack of distance. The locality to which I belonged sometimes weighed on me during participant observation, directing my attention to less interesting aspects of the research. I took for granted key community behaviours, almost completely ignoring them when planning my work. I still had to take into account the natural desire among people to whitewash their surroundings, to defend 'their own' from the gaze of 'outsiders'. As an ethnographer, I was obliged to present them reflexively and with an anthropological frame of mind. And I had an obligation to represent them well.

Because of all this, the opinions of people from outside the field were an invaluable help to me. Meetings with my thesis supervisor helped to shape my work, to focus on the most important issues, sometimes at the expense of abandoning others. Conversations with other MA students helped to see more clearly what was happening in my field.

When describing a familiar organization, the help of other ethnographers can prove precious and sometimes necessary. Considering the opinions of others about the material we have collected can prove as important as the research methods we use.

There are, however, some fundamentally important ethical issues that ethnographers must take very seriously indeed. The imperative of being there, experiencing the field first hand is the crucial source of an ethnographer's claim to knowledge (Pachirat 2018). Failing to do that or upholding an engagement that is lacking is reason enough to disqualify any study calling itself ethnographic. The example in Box 6.2 shows the importance of presence and how it leads to both methodological and ethical dilemmas. An ethnographer is never just a detached and disinterested scientist but an active, moral and epistemological presence.

The ethnographic study depends on the quality of relationships established in the field. These are ruled by a situational ethics, emergent and multifaceted and thus impossible to plan or predict but with an imperative to adapt, adjust and become trustworthy in the field (Wästerfors 2019). As David Wästerfors explains, it would be much easier to establish the depth of the researcher's ethical engagement if one had access to his notes, than by reading the final textual report. However, notes are private as is everything that contains any notion whatsoever that could endanger the anonymity of the field. That is a principal ethical obligation of ethnography – which is a study of social and cultural processes, not individual people or organizations. The identity of the research participants must be kept secret. That includes documents such as ethical procedure and funding papers which, unfortunately, are often made accessible to colleagues. Wästerfors mentions an occasion when the identity of his field has been revealed in this way, to detrimental effects. The difficult issue is how to reconcile these two imperatives. It is clear that ethical forms cannot provide a solution to this dilemma. We agree with Bob Simpson (2011) that what is most beneficial here are discussions within the close ethnographic community. Everyone within the community is equally obliged to protect the identity of the own and each other's field but peers are both keeping an eye out to safeguard research honesty and ready and competent to advise each other.

Furthermore, it is not just a methodological but a moral obligation to strive at good representation of the field, doing it justice (Wästerfors 2019). Karolina Walatek, the author of the study presented in Box 6.2, was intensely aware of this duty, both because the interviewees reminded her of it, and because she, as an ex-insider herself, was particularly sensitive to the identity and representational needs of her field. Quite often, during her fieldwork, she reported what she experienced as expectations of her interviewees and moral dilemmas deriving from them. Simpson (2011) speaks of the ethical moment occurring when the ethnographer starts describing his field. Writing in a responsible way relies on a number of decisions of what to reveal and what to conceal on ethical grounds. The ethnographer is a moral agent, in terms of Levinasian ethics: 'the skill of the ethnographer lies in the developing and managing relations founded on trust, respect and an avoidance of delimiting the subject' (Simpson 2011: 385). As Karolina's supervisor, I am aware of how much of the material she decided not to reveal, even if some of it was very interesting and could potentially make her contribution stronger.

6.3 PRINCIPLES OF REPRESENTATION

Finally, let us consider the question of representation. What and whom do ethnographies represent? Unlike quantitative research, ethnography does not aspire to representing populations. The lack of random sampling makes it impossible to generalize results from ethnographic research this way. However, qualitative research is longitudinal and usually well suited for the exploration of processes and dynamics. This is particularly true about ethnography, which often takes several years in one given field. Organization theorist Tony Watson (2011) calls this mode of representation knowledge, 'how things work'. It consists of looking for patterns of behaviour that emerge over time, revealing relative rather than absolute truths. These patterns may very well take the shape of emerging stories (Czarniawska 1999).

BOX 6.3   STORIES ABOUT COMMUNICATION, BY
                 MARTA SZELUGA-ROMAŃSKA

My main research problem concerned the organizing aspects of different
managers' communication processes. How does the managers' communication 'organize' an organization's practices and behaviours? As an ethnographer, I set out in the field full of energy and curiosity but realized soon
enough that this was a highly challenging endeavour. I found myself to be
a researcher of complexity: both communication and managerial roles are
multidimensional. To explore them requires not just qualitative methods
but also a lot of reflexivity and ongoing conversations with other ethnographers. Luckily, I always had great support from my wonderful mentor.

I carried out recurrent and in-depth interviews with 15 interlocutors:
managers from business, governmental and non-profit organizations. The
average time of each interview was about an hour. The transcriptions took
124 pages of the text. I also conducted observations and used my notes to
develop my knowledge. Furthermore, I analysed informal and published
documents from each researched organization. It took me a year before
all the pieces of the puzzle fell into place for me: from a simple reading
through of the material, via categorizing of gathered data and their analysis,
to conclusions and models.

At first, I felt inundated by the research material: facts, narratives, examples of organizational 'adventures', humour, technical instructions, descriptions of encounters and conversations with other people, etc. All in all, I was
presented with a mixture of overlapping plots. In some respects part of them
felt somehow similar but mostly different. One simple example: I asked
each manager how do they prefer to be addressed by other employees: by
their first name, by family name, Mr/Mrs/Ms, or maybe 'chief', a form that
is actually in use in the conversational Polish language. They all offered
me not just a simple answer but some kind of complex narrative. After the
analysis of this material, it was clear to me that there was no coherence in
it. Everyone seemed to prefer a different form and they presented me with
various stories justifying why they did so. For example an interviewee had
had some bad experiences from the past and was abused because he allowed
people to call him by his first name. Someone else claimed it was completely situational but then went on to detail how it depended on the particular
person or situation. Another listed his own rules: he let employees call him
by his name only if the age difference was less than 20 years. But in this
lack of patterns there was nonetheless a pattern on a different level: people
create elaborate justification for such a simple thing as how they want to be
addressed.

My aim was to organize the research material in a way enabling analysis. The first step was to set categories, the second to link separated categories into a summarizing model. In the presented example the emerging category was 'justification of address'. The form is attached to something more than just the function of addressing someone. There is a story and a plot leading to one preference or another. Taken together, this is a plot all by itself. But what kind of plot? It took me some time to see it.

For me, the moment I realized the importance of plots behind the plots occurred when I spoke with a parish priest. He was a manager of his parish yet he used a different language and offered different justifications. Yet he too went into great length to justify all of the simplest details of his communication style with his employees. Communication was important for each of my interviewees, but it did not have to be 'managed' in a similar way. It was the priest who, using the least managerialist language of them all, was able to express the moral significance of organizational communication. And it then turned out that this is, indeed, a common plot in all the stories I heard: the process of making moral sense of communication.

After long hours of re-listening to the record and re-reading of the transcriptions, I realized that the plot was predominantly a moral one. The puzzles clicked into their proper places.

The example in Box 6.3 shows how Marta Szeluga-Romańska focused on stories and narrative threads that emerged from her field. Listening and re-listening to the interviews, she began to see that there were plots on different levels. At one point she saw some larger plots behind the more superficial ones. Then other plots began to emerge. Barbara Czarniawska (1999) points out that stories have plots: a plot is the strategy of the text that leads from one point of equilibrium to another. It leads through a number of developments to more stable conditions. Lists or chronologies are not stories because they lack a plot that would connect events in a meaningful way. Stories are ways of making sense of social reality, provide meaning and strive towards an understanding of what is going on (Weick 1995). In Marta Szeluga-Romańska's research, repetitive stories drew her attention to patterns explaining how her field understood and enacted managerial communication, not always on a superficially narrative level. Stories do not necessarily aim at finding causal connections in the positivist meaning of the word, but present intentions and actions. In other words, they show who undertook which actions and the consequences these actions had, or 'how things work'.

Paul Willis (2000), discussing the question of representation in ethnography, proposes a broad metaphor of life as art. He reminds us that it is a living thing, representing something that holds true for human experience and argues that there exists an ethnographically imagined possibility to link life and art in order to help us make sense of our everyday experience. The representation does not have to, indeed, cannot, be immediate and direct, but it should be able to offer some understanding of some of the relevant meanings. Social reality itself is composed partly of representations (Willis 2000: 77), they are meaning systems. The role of the ethnographer is to observe them in the form of meaningful patterns and re-tell them for their audiences, translate them, to bring opportunities for knowledge, self-knowledge and control (Willis 2000: 77). In other words, it is a relevant representation which helps the readers to learn about processes of everyday symbolic work in contexts which they can either recognize or use for development of knowledge about the human side of social life. Like Willis, we believe that this can have important even if not necessarily immediate effects for human enlightenment and emancipation.

NOTE

1. Available at: https://www.artsteps.com/embed/60af9f829dfcccacded6a5d3/560/315

7.   Why ethnography?

7.1   SOME WARNINGS

Ethnography allows exploring new and unknown territories. Its direct contact with the field, emerging research design and being open to serendipities and surprises make ethnography an excellent approach to looking at well-known research fields and problems from a novel perspective. In this chapter, we will show in which areas ethnography proved to be especially valuable.

Ethnography is one of many established research tools social scientists use. By widening the scope of available tools that we are comfortable with, we are avoiding formulating research problems in a way that calls for one specific method only. The researcher's bias is well expressed by a catchphrase: *if the only tool you have is a hammer, you treat everything as if it were a nail.* Sometimes this bias is called the law of the instrument. Mastering diverse instruments allow us to produce more nuanced results than when we only pound with a hammer. In this chapter, we show in which circumstances ethnography is the right methodological choice. For some researchers ethnography can be an additional method. However, for others, ethnography becomes the researchers' main and only approach. If that is the case, we strongly suggest not treating it as a method (because it can become a proverbial hammer), but as a holistic approach, a way of being in the field and as a way of learning from it.

Holistic ethnographers tend to call themselves just *ethnographers,* rather than social scientists or researchers. Holistic ethnography informs the research situation, the engagement of the researcher and perhaps also her identity. First, it is a form of methodological honesty. The law of the instrument indicates that methodological pluralism often turns out to be only declarative. Ethnographers explicitly limit their choices. Second, ethnography is more than just another tool. It is a methodological tradition shaped by the interaction between theory and research practice. Last, ethnography is a very intensive and engaging practice that requires devoting more time than other methods. When your research engages, for an extended period, not only your whole life but also your close ones, it is hard to tread it just as another tool one might use in the future. Once initiated into ethnography, researchers keep mastering their skills.

Ethnographers may be regarded as social scientists holding only one tool in their hands. Similarly, a blacksmith is only pounding away with a hammer.

However, calling a hammer a limiting factor in the blacksmith's hand would not be a good evaluation of his labour. The results of their work may be diverse, practical or artistic, simple or complex. However, nobody expects a wooden table or a pair of shoes from them. Blacksmiths work with hammers and metal in their forge. Ethnographers in turn produce ethnography. Their forge would be the academic community, the body of literature, and theories.

Not everyone who occasionally uses ethnography calls themselves an ethnographer. However, often trying ethnography leads to becoming an ethnographer. Why use ethnography, or why be an ethnographer? What are the possible motivations to choose this path, and what are the consequences? We answer these questions regarding epistemological, practical, career, political, identity, and emotional levels. We address diverse, non-academic perspectives because, in real life, an individual deciding on details of a project considers only strictly methodological aspects. In practice, choosing ethnography over other methods is not a result of rational analysis that can be done according to a specific model. It is then essential to discuss when to use ethnography and when it is not a good choice. Consequently, we decided to include the relative weaknesses of ethnography and possible negative consequences of applying the method.

Let us start with a warning. Ethnography may not be a good choice for some researchers because of its high involvement and identity-building power. Many of us enjoy being ethnographers. Devotion in research is very good and we need genuine motivation. However, fanaticism is a serious risk for social scientists. There exist people who develop an almost exclusivist zeal and are not willing to give up on ethnography and promote it, no matter what. This dedication to ethnographic method and identity is evident among researchers practising ethnography commercially in industry. As one of us has shown in a text written with another co-author (Krzyworzeka and Rodak 2013), the main aim of anthropologists entering business practice was to do ethnography. It was manifested in the way they prepared offers where a fundamental value proposition was the use of ethnography or when they were fighting to include the term anthropologist or ethnographer in their job titles. Their organizations also demanded loyalty and responsibility. However, with some ethnographers, there is no splitting of loyalties – something which we consider necessary for an ethical approach. One should be loyal and devoted to the ethnographic community as well as the field or other social settings one takes part in. A one-sided engagement leads to moral tension, which tends to be experienced by the fanatic ethnographers as a source of frustration. Ethnographic practice and community offer a strong identity that may result in evangelizing that often is not needed or welcomed. Being initiated into ethnography and taking the initiation too religiously may make one look down at other methods – and human beings. Beware!

To counterweight the warning, we would like to point out one practical aspect of ethnography that we both especially enjoy. Fieldwork and interactions with research participants are a good source of energy, inspiration and motivation that help us continue the project. To ignite the passion for research and maintain it, we encourage students to start fieldwork as early as possible, even before the literature review and formulating precise research questions. This teaching approach is not recognized by more traditionally oriented researchers. However, we continue sending students to meet the field early because of the positive motivational and methodological results this practice offers. Discussing theories in a classroom and reading literature in a library constitute the foundation of a good ethnography. However, these 'armchair' activities may sometime drain students' energy and willingness to continue the project. Based on our observations, students are more engaged in interacting with literature when they have previous field experience. The history of ethnography teaches that encountering the field can profoundly transform even carefully designed research problems – which is the correct approach in inductive research! The ethnography process is iterative, and research design is evolving. If our field is not hard to access, we may want to start our interaction with the field at an early stage. In ethnography, it makes a lot of sense to move the initial contact with the field, if possible, earlier in the research process. In other qualitative methods, it would be somewhat better to stick to the procedure, first literature review, then empirical research, and finally data analysis and interpretation.

Practising ethnography is uplifting, but this otherwise positive characteristic may lead an individual too far in their engagement, resulting in unfavourable results for the project or the person. We discussed the hazards of ethnography in Chapter 1, *Entering the field*, here, we add another risk that is not field-related but results from the intensive nature of some fieldwork that makes the ethnographer *forget* their bodies. As a result, researchers, such as the activists in high-commitment organizations (Elidrissi and Courpasson 2021), experience physical and emotional fatigue or even breakdowns. Some consequences of too intensive an ethnography threaten not the project's aims but also the researcher.

Going native is a term describing crossing from participant observation onto participation only. The transition undermines the ability to practice ethnography. The ethnographer becomes a group member, internalizing the group's values, culture, and way of life to such an extent that she loses the ability to reflect and analyse her experience. It is an important warning that the ethnographic community shares stories about ethnographers who went native, but *going native* rarely happens.[1] We should be aware of the risks, but this threat indicates the core of ethnography's strength – a deep and multidimensional bond with the field.

Deep involvement has become a distinctive characteristic of ethnography. When ethnographic research was founded, participation was not a choice but a necessity because of the remoteness and high degree of the otherness of the first groups studied by anthropologists. Ethnography is still well-suited to study unknown groups, even if they are not living on other continents but are a next-door newly emerged social phenomena. Let's suppose we approach in turn a well-known phenomenon ethnographically, which is a more recent strategy. In that case, we can make the familiar unfamiliar and look at something that we know well, even our group, in a novel way. The Inuit nation was a remote and unknown field only to the first generations of ethnographers who studied people living in the North. However, the academic body of knowledge about Inuit culture is now quite rich and well-established. The specific problem of suicide among the Inuit was also not a new phenomenon for social scientists when Lisa Stevenson (Stevenson 2014) got interested in this topic in the second decade of the twenty-first century. She managed to tell an untold and unseen story about life and death in the Canadian Arctic. Stevenson focused her ethnographic attention on hesitation, on what is uncertain to her research participant. As a result, she reinterpreted the meaning of suicide in the Canadian Arctic by offering a novel but troubling account of the Inuit's experience of time and death. Ethnographic research allowed Stevenson to reinterpret the politics of care deployed for decades by the state administration. The Canadian administration aimed at minimizing the number of deaths among the Inuit. Protecting other people's lives is undoubtedly a key value. However, Stevenson also shows that when pursuing that humanitarian aims, the administration deprived the Inuit of essential elements of their life for them. The state activities destroyed social and spiritual worlds, focusing on protecting physical existence. Ethnographic new interpretations of saving human life practices may even shock a reader outside the studied community.

BOX 7.1   THE THORNY ISSUE OF RISK IN ETHNOGRAPHIC RESEARCH: PERCEPTION, PREJUDICE AND UNINTENDED CONSEQUENCES?, BY CORRETTER ONGUS AND TOM VINE

Corretter is a Kenyan national currently studying for her PhD at a British university. Corretter's research explores the degree to which language, culture and belief shape investment decision-making within rural communities in Kenya. In particular, Corretter is interested in the extent to which the grammatical structures of the various languages spoken in Kenya (some of which do not have future tenses) constrain speakers from conceptualizing future events, and hence, constrain the impact of investment decisions. Tom is Corretter's primary supervisor.

For Kohn and Shore (2017) research is an intrinsically risky enterprise. In a bid to enhance our understanding, ethnographers must step (literally) into the unknown. Early in 2022, Corretter submitted her ethics application for this research. The official response to the application contained 21 separate recommendations, including some specific questions. An excerpt from this letter is presented below.

> You clearly identified some of the risks [inherent to this research]. However, the majority of the Committee expressed concern about levels of risk and… would like to know how these would be mitigated […] You will be travelling to unknown places sometimes without chaperone:
> i. Please advise how it would be known where you would be going?
> ii. Who would know your itinerary?
> iii. How could it be known whether you were safe?
> iv. What measures would you put in place to ensure your safety?

While the University's ethics committee will no doubt have the best interests of their students in mind (and safety is of course paramount), both Corretter and Tom felt that the nature of the formal response begs a broader enquiry in respect of perceived vis-à-vis actual risk, unconscious prejudice, and unanticipated consequences. There was an overwhelming sense that the perception of risk in Kenya shared by the ethics committee was at odds with the reality. The suggestion, for example, that Corretter would be travelling to 'unknown places' not only reinforces the outdated idea that non-Western cultures are alien and should – perhaps – be feared, but it was actually incorrect. This is because Corretter is from Kenya. Following receipt of this official response, she commented to Tom: 'Kenya is my home; it is where I feel safest!' On reflection, Corretter and Tom wondered whether they would have received different recommendations had Corretter's fieldwork been planned for, say, Australia or the United States (ironically, these would have been alien cultures in Corretter's eyes). Beyond the apparent ethnocentric bias contained in the letter, there is – perhaps – an unconscious sexism, too: 'You will be travelling to unknown places sometimes without chaperone'. Again, had Corretter been male, would the letter have been concerned about the absence of a chaperone?

Corretter and Tom have no desire to cast aspersions. And there is, of course, a sense that the ethics committee is compelled to retain a focus on safety above and beyond all other considerations, including social sensitivities. However, what was – perhaps – most notable about the letter was its potential for unintended consequences. As we began to re-draft the ethics application, Corretter commented to Tom: 'I was really looking forward to my fieldwork, but this ethics process has made me apprehensive about it.'

Note: Due to the topic of this chapter we asked for a third person voice, to tackle the difficult and thorny questions of prejudice and bias of perception.

7.2 SOME REASSURANCES

The social life of the contemporary human being has become more and more fragmented and specialized. Professions, subcultures, and social movements emerge around us at an increasing pace. New groups stop identifying themselves with old established social worlds and detach themselves from them. They start establishing their institutions and communications platforms to promote new claims. The changing social landscape constantly creates something that we would like to understand better. Applying ethnography to study something new and unknown, as it used to be historically adopted, appears as a natural methodological choice. And yet novel phenomena are ephemeral and may quickly disappear. For example, some online communities and platforms may not be there anymore when the research project is over. Ethnography is slow, and so ethnographers are motivated to learn something that extends beyond the pure interest in the new shiny object. Ethnography can also be used to study the familiar, not only the unknown. The method gives a fresh perspective on old social worlds and cultures that have been around for a long time, and we already know what to expect from them. It is a quest for surprises.

Furthermore, ethnographers often study such perennial elements as food, clothes, kinship, or boredom. They are fundamental but mundane aspects of our life, and the fact that people take them for granted makes those elements of our life especially good to study ethnographically. In her study of boredom, Andrea Matošević (2021) was trying to grasp the imponderability of actual life in Pula, the Croatian city. She closely examined the language people used in their everyday experiences. Especially important was one word, *tapija*, which was not recorded, codified or institutionalized. As a part of the vernacular, however, it plays a vital role in expressing the philosophy of doing nothing. Matošević, by studying boredom, tells us a story of the situated Gramscian philosophical system of spontaneous philosophy.

A strength that is rarely acknowledged but, in our opinion, is important, is the versatility of ethnography. Ethnography can be fruitfully used in combination with other methods. New perspectives that researchers discover during fieldwork, when applied to historical documents and even statistical data, result in novel research questions and fresh interpretations. Lisa Stevenson's observations of Inuit's current life had some detrimental effects due to policymakers' strong reaction, but they also paved the way to reinterpret historical documents. Ethnography extends beyond the present, as in William Reddy's

(2001) study on the French Revolution. The ethnographic ways of looking at emotions influenced Reddy's historical inquiry. The cultural aspects of emotions, not the dominating psychological perspective, allowed Reddy to shed new light on Jacobinism that, in his interpretation, contradicted the previously existing emotional regime. Sometimes, however, ethnography forms partnerships with much younger and distant cousins than history. Ethnography offers a unique type of academic objectivity that resides at the level of all ethnographies, not a single one (Hymes 1996). Ethnographers operate in other scientists' community, which spans time and space. We learn to value the community because we are keenly aware that our experience and research are partial. Ethnographers need to learn from other fields to understand their own better. Things that are real and important but unrecognized are not just possible but natural research topics of ethnographers. For example Jenny Helin (2020) proposes 'going deeper' and 'flying high' in texts by letting the narrative from the field evolve into a writing-temporality meshwork. Such temporality is not one-dimensional, and brings a possibility to express 'a moment of being human where opposing forces of darkness and light meet' (Helin 2020: 8). Anna Giza and Monika Kostera (in progress) are putting together a book out of the unused ethnographic material they have collected during their professional lives. When they discussed these omissions they realized that there was a large overarching theme that constituted a frame for all the plots, themes and ideas that Polish journals and publishers had tended to dismiss – the transition from state socialism to capitalism of the 1990s. Most social studies do not age well and especially quantitative studies, albeit ethnographic material, once interpreted in a way that exposes the dynamics and patterns, is more like Saint Saturnin wines than like apple juice. It acquires character.

Ethnography has the capacity to reveal what often goes unseen not just in everyday life but oftentimes in social science research. Doing fieldwork is simple but not easy. Ethnographic practice is just an extension of the ability to learn a culture, a skill everyone possesses. Ethnographers study things that every human being learns: norms, meanings, and patterns. What then makes ethnography specific? The ability to reflect on participation is what differentiates ethnography from learning a culture by a layperson. Ethnographers are not just academics but they often work as journalists, non-fiction authors, travellers, and missionaries who explore other cultures also without 'going native'. They are able to see the human side of many, if not most, phenomena. Contrary to so many contemporary trends, they do not treat the human being as a means to any end – but as an end in itself. They are the modern humanists.

Ethnography as social science is, at the same time, reflective and practical. Ethnographers who are also academics not only reflect on their practice and engage in academic debate, but take part in the practical work of *doing* ethnography. Their main aim is to offer new ideas and contribute to our understanding of humankind. It used to be relatively easy to make an original contribution to knowledge by describing a relatively unknown group or one that was never studied before. However, as Evans-Pritchard said, it would be just factual knowledge and

> anyone who is not a complete idiot can do fieldwork... Anyone can produce a new fact; the thing is to produce a new idea. (Evans-Pritchard 1976: 243)

Researchers working toward producing new ideas are inspired and guided by theories, apply academic apparatus, and engage in dialogue with the academic community.

Ethnographers usually spend a prolonged time in the field, often becoming domain experts. The practice leads to gaining detailed knowledge about the studied area. It may be a first-hand, nuanced knowledge about an industry, country, region, or the ability to communicate with locals effectively. This expertise is being used outside academia by companies, non-governmental organizations, and governmental institutions. Ethnographers' knowledge goes beyond what they wrote in publications. It is also an implicit knowledge, know-how, and know-who that cannot easily be transferred into the text but can be used in practice. Because of the specificity of ethnographic expertise gained in close, trust-based interactions with research participants, with that knowledge comes big responsibility. The American Anthropological Association's code of ethics starts with the 'do not harm' principle but requires anthropologists to make research findings accessible. The latter principle is especially valid in commercial applications when companies require exclusive results. However, the most discussed was the engagement of anthropologists and other social scientists in the US military's Human Terrain System project, where researchers were embedded in military teams in Iraq and Afghanistan in the first decade of the twenty-first century. This engagement of anthropologists raised concerns over all Code of Ethics and posed problems for non-affiliated military researchers working in this and other regions. Ethnographers become experts in broader areas of their study, not only in narrow topics of interest. For example, in researching the performances of sales representatives in Multi-level marketing (MLM) organizations, an ethnographer must study diverse aspects of the field, such as the historical development of the phenomenon and examples from other geographic regions. Going beyond the selling interaction, an ethnographer would be interested in the financial aspects of this practice and private social relations. Ethnography encourages taking the holistic approach as ethnographers gain a broad knowledge of the field. However, the use of that knowledge outside the academic context is limited.

Reading this chapter, one may get the impression that ethnography promises more than other methods. It is because it is more than a method and should be evaluated as such.[2] It is more than a method because it is impossible to discuss just data gathering techniques separately. The practice of fieldwork unites with theorizing. The ethnography of both distant cultures as well as mundane settings such as workplaces and organizations serves as an excellent example of this union. Earlier conceptualizations used to limit and reify such social settings in ways that contradicted human experience. The project described in Box 7.2 seems to be located somewhere between the familiar and the 'exotic' and is an example of intensive ethnographic sense-making by the researchers.

BOX 7.2   LEARNING THE LANGUAGE OF MUSIC, BY ANNA PRUSZYŃSKA AND MIKOŁAJ MAŁECKI

Music is a popular and interesting topic for ethnographic research. We chose a small but well regarded Polish symphony orchestra. We had no preconceptions and not much prior musical education; however, we like listening to music.

Not being professional musicians, we could not engage in participant observation during rehearsals, even if the musicians allowed us to. But we conducted direct observation. During the concert, as members of the audience, we regarded ourselves as active participants, enjoying the music. The knowledge of the instruments and basic musical notions (such as pianissimo or rallentando) made us particularly attentive audience members.

Our observation covered three orchestra rehearsals, including a dress rehearsal, and a concert. We watched the orchestra, sitting among the musicians and watching them from different places. We were sitting behind the harp, next to the double basses, and in the audience. The study ended with a conversation with one of the musicians. The conversation helped us to make sense of much of what we saw and a main thematic axis then emerged: whether musicians belong to one or two worlds – art or craft.

The worlds turned out to be amenable. The same instrumentalists sometimes regarded being placed in one and then the other. It depends on their function in a given musical piece at a given moment. More often, they seem to remain in the domain of craftsmanship. The transition to the world of art occurs when the piece allows a given instrumentalist to come to the fore for a moment. Then the engagement in playing and freedom of interpretation increase, and the performed music becomes art. Such a sudden transition from the world of art to the world of craftsmanship has consequences for the whole orchestra, which must then adapt to the 'momentary' soloist. Also, the conductor then focuses her attention on such a person, making sure, for example, that nothing disturbs her playing.

In addition, the spatial position divides the orchestra into performative musical 'worlds': there is a centre–periphery axis. The centre is closest to the conductor and directly in front of her. The periphery are those who are furthest from the conductor and concertmaster and those who occupy the seats at the sides of the orchestra. It is more likely to move into the world of art when sitting at the centre.

The conductor plays a key role in the work of the orchestra. However, she is neither a boss nor an integral part of the ensemble. Each programme may be conducted by a different maestro, who must come to an agreement with the musicians each time. The conductor engages in intensive emotional work. She plays the role of a kind of a 'guardian spirit' of the ensemble, taking care of the well-being of its members (every critical remark is counterbalanced with an anecdote or a compliment) or, for example, that the horn players are guaranteed appropriate breaks for breathing during their playing. The conductor also shows the musicians what to focus on at a given moment, who is leading the melody, whose part is the most difficult at a given point, etc. She was saying things such as: 'let's help the flutes in this devilishly difficult part', 'let's be colleagues for each other', 'the strings are supposed to rest here'. Her job is also to convey to the orchestra the feelings they should put into the piece.

The conductor used words and gestures. The musicians used their music to communicate. The orchestra is a powerful communication system. However, we did not get the impression that there is some mysterious and completely incomprehensible system of communication operating inside the orchestra based on professional knowledge of classical and symphonic music principles. Even if we probably did not catch much of the musical signs, facial expressions and gestures seemed largely comprehensible to us. Sitting among the musicians felt as being part of a communication of emotions related to the piece being performed.

7.3   A HUMAN METHOD

BOX 7.3   IS IT REALLY WORTH IT?, BY ANNA (ANIA) LEWANDOWSKA

I love qualitative methods because of the depth and the context one can grasp by using them. But let's be honest, it is a little scary when you have to go out into the field and spend time interviewing someone or stand observing a social situation, while feeling awkward and out of place. Quantitative methods are much more comfortable. You don't have to feel stressed out due to saying something wrong, feel the sweat coming down your forehead. You have already prepared the questionnaire and if you are lucky, you don't have to meet any people, by just uploading it online.

So when I decided to use qualitative interviews and non-participant observation for my bachelor thesis I knew I was up for a challenge. I decided to interview civil servants in a municipal office. The topic was emotional labour and the general difficulties that clerks face in their job.

One important detail of the study was that I had been employed at the same office before, so I knew people. At first I thought it would make things easier, right? But I couldn't be more wrong. Since I knew the people it was much more awkward to just stand and observe them doing their job without participating. But the biggest challenge was to interview them. When I asked questions about the specifics of their jobs they usually said something like: 'But you know it already', or just restricted their answers. My first interview lasted no more than 20 minutes and I was afraid that all of them would be that short. But then I got an idea to ask people I knew to introduce me to other departments in which I haven't met anyone. And then it clicked. People were more eager to tell fascinating stories about their encounters with clients and, since I was introduced by other employees, they trusted me more. Another problem was ethical. It's hard to separate your own feelings and experiences from what you are studying to be a real researcher. But after reading books and articles I knew it was all about mindset and creating a border between Ania 'The Former Employee' and Ania 'The Sociologist'.

One more issue arose when the people I was supposed to interview didn't want to do it in their free time or outside the office. I had to do it during their work time and get permission from their supervisor. The interviews also had to be stopped when they had clients in and some of them were in groups of two to three people. Even though it added a lot of work for me, it also had some unexpected results. First, I got the opportunity to observe some interactions with clients, which are important in understanding emotional labour done by clerks. And second the group interviews allowed for people to open up more and complement each other's stories.

The ethnographer is a human being, among human beings. It makes it harder to do this kind of research but it is also more rewarding.

Qualitative methods require a lot of unforeseen work, but they also force you to be creative. And in my opinion, if you can solve such problems on the spot, you are a good researcher. All interviews and observations were different and each one added so much to my study. It was honestly one of the most gratifying feelings!

Ethnography is a way to understand what it means to be human. We can use ethnography to address fundamental questions about humanity. But it is not the only academic tradition preoccupied with this question. *What it means to be human* does not only sound philosophical but is one of the most fundamental questions for ethnographers. The vignette by Anna Lewandowska (Box 7.3) shows how a novice ethnographer uses ethnography to collect human stories and become more creative. She also remarks on the human requirements: ethics and honesty. It is a demanding way of doing research but Anna feels it is worth it.

Philosophers are helping us understand the human condition through thinking that elevates us to an abstract and transcendent level. What is an ethnographic contribution to this thousand years-long line of practising thinking? Ethnography addressing the same questions is descending into the everyday (Jackson 2012). Furthermore, ethnography practised as empirical philosophy combines the universal with the particular. As a result, it offers a perspective that emerges from your world to 'explore *empirically* the lived experience of actual people in everyday situations before venturing suggestions as to what human beings may have in common' (Jackson 2012: 9, emphasis in original). We can read philosophy and poetry when we want to broaden our understanding of the human condition. Or we can conduct ethnography, a kind of deep experiment practised on ourselves, in a controlled manner. As ethnographers, we throw ourselves into the field where we cannot be fully ourselves and are displaced from our customary ways of thinking and acting. This displacement creates an opportunity to look at ourselves from the standpoint of another. Ethnography puts us into uncomfortable situations that we would not have placed ourselves in otherwise. Ethnography promises, if not guarantees, an unusual experience, as the main requirement of this research asks to leave your world behind. The mental move, unlike in philosophy, requires ethnographers to put themselves into positions when they feel emotional turmoil, moral confusion, and often physical disturbance. If not motivated and guided by ethnographic principles, we would probably not force ourselves to suspend our worldview. Ethnography as empirical philosophy allows us to move intellectually from our own to others' positions through displacing our whole selves from typical routines of thinking and acting (Jackson 2012). Jackson suggests that Hermes stands between 'different countries of the mind' and as a patron of thieves, travellers, and heralds would suit well also as a patron of ethnographers. Further, Jackson asks what value derives from this transgression. To answer that, 'oracular wisdom requires unsettling and questioning what we customarily take for granted or consider true'. Moreover, 'value of doubt, for it is through the loss of firm belief that one stands to gain a sense of belonging to a pluralistic world whose horizons are open' (Jackson 2012: 11). This self-imposed displacement is used not only in academic research. A fresh perspective on well-known topics became urgent and a priority in business practice when competition and innovations accelerated. Even in abbreviated form, both in time and intellectual depth, ethnography turns out to be valued in innovation, design and marketing activities. Many current approaches to designing things, processes, and services have in common that they suspend thinking about solutions. They instead start with a good problem statement and understanding of the user. Often this approach is called a user-centred design. Getting to know the user and gaining empathy are prerequisites for working on a novel product. And here, ethnography comes to help get inspiration directly from the field. The prime example of such use of ethnography in business practice may be design thinking. This approach to solving problems innovatively became extremely popular in the last decade.

One of the publications about creating innovations developed in the design thinking stream identifies being an anthropologist as being one out of ten faces of an innovator (Kelley and Littman 2005). Anthropologists' main appeal is that they are skilled at reframing problems in a new way. The ethnographic practice delivers a crucial component in the innovation process. The authors codified ethnographic input for innovations into six points. People in this role

> practice the Zen principle of 'beginner's mind.'
> embrace human behavior with all its surprises
> draw inferences by listening to their intuition
> seek out epiphanies through a sense of 'Vuja De.'
> are willing to search for clues in the trash bin
> keep 'bug lists' or 'idea wallets'.
> (Kelley and Littman 2005: 17–19)

This list describes ethnographic practices well, most of which we discussed in an academic context. Ethnographers are willing to put aside what they know to observe with an open mind. They are trying to understand human life through the practice of empathy to observe without judging. They are also able to see things that, until the day, remain unnoticed. The authors use the term that is the opposite of déjà vu. The 'Vuja De' expresses the sense of seeing something for the first time, even if what we observe comes from the nearest, well-known reality. One way of achieving that is through searching for understanding in unusual places and looking for the non-obvious. In design research, looking into a trash bin is often literal. The first five points can be applied to academic contexts. The last one, however, seems specific to the field of innovation. The innovator anthropologist is recording things from everyday life that surprise them because they do not work correctly and seem broken. The thing that bugs them is recorded on the bug list, creative concepts worth development and problems worth solving end up in the idea wallet.

However, ethnographic research also makes us realize that innovations are overrated and that what is condemned as 'resistance to change' is a healthy reaction of employees and organizations towards managerial pressures to innovate, which may at times be unsustainable. Helena Fornstedt (2021) conducted a multi-sited ethnographic study of key employees responsible for innovation, managers, engineers, and specialists, employed at a major international supplier of high voltage product called BigE in her narrative. She reveals that 'resistance to change' is a complex and multifaceted process, consisting of many different behaviours and attitudes, which help people to adapt to the innovation project. In other words, if a company wishes to innovate (which is by no means always the best option), they should be respectful of resistance processes, because they actually form part the innovation. So, ethnography is practical in many ways and senses. It is judicious to consult an ethnographic study before making simplified decisions.

However, there are two main obstacles to the practice-oriented use of ethnographic knowledge about a mundane field. Learning from ethnographers differs from the learning that 'experts' offer. First, for many practitioners, especially in for-profit business organizations, learning from ethnography requires too much effort and time. Ethnography does not provide precise answers in a compact, easily digestible form. In contrast, experts that usually inform business practice offer persuasive, practical, action-oriented knowledge. Second, those in power to make changes in the field are not always those with whom ethnographers would like to share the findings. Additionally, ethnographers may not be interested in further close interactions with their study field. Post-fieldwork loss of interest can happen when research is motivated by a high degree of the otherness of the area. That otherness may manifest itself in a lack of understanding of the internal logic of a group, which may lead to irritation or even fear of the group, like a mafia, extremist political groups, and religious cults. Negative emotions toward a group can motivate the researcher to explore that field ethnographically to gain a better understanding and grasp the native point of view. Often, groups' otherness is enhanced by stereotypes that are the primary source of knowledge about the group. When faced with irritation on a specific group, ethnographers may read this emotion as a sign that outsiders' knowledge about the group is limited. However, even if an ethnography can help grasp the native point of view, we may want to leave the organization after the project. When their values, when even better understood by us, are still contradictory to our values. For example, if we see that an organization contributes to someone's suffering, their actions are harmful. Even if a more profound understanding may differ from our initial preconceptions, the results may push an ethnographer further from this group to a more critical stance. For example, a student ethnographer decided to study a far-right youth organization ethnographically. She discovered the key role a written text played in building the relations between organization members. Her understanding of the organization was not stereotypical anymore, but how the texts are used is still oppressive to exercising symbolic power (Zagrzejewska 2008).

Returning to Zofia Sokolewicz's idea of ethnography, what does this little book do? It is up to you, the reader, to decide. But we have been hoping to do something: to invite lots of people, yourselves, our ex-students and colleagues, our own selves from different times. We believe Zofia would have approved and said that it is only by engaging in conversation back and forth about who we are and what we do as ethnographers that we truly become a collective: *the ethnographers*.[3] And that is how we organize, how we lay the foundations (Zofia liked the idea of ideas and values as foundations of structures) of ethnographic science.

So here is an idea: in this book we wanted to show that ethnography is the best methodological choice when we want to challenge established worldviews: to explore what it means to be human. Ethnography is for those situations when we are open to surprises when our aim is not, as in most of the other methods, verifying precise ideas and understanding through reduction. Instead, ethnography inspires, ignites the imagination, and deepens understanding rather than verifies facts. The biggest appeal of ethnography is its ambition to represent the reality of a patchwork of overlapping activities without unnecessary simplification. Ethnography is for those who would like to build a kaleidoscope, not a powerful magnifying glass.

NOTES

1. Although sometimes it does, see the story in Box 2.1.
2. If you are enjoying this chapter, we recommend that you read Gaggiotti, Kostera and Krzyworzeka (2017) entitled 'More than a method?'. The title contains a question, and the answer is, as you may guess, a resounding yes. But there are some good ethnographic stories in the paper, as well.
3. She liked to point this out, for example, in one of her last published texts dedicated to Polish anthropologist Cezaria Baudouin de Courtenay (Sokolewicz 2019). She talks of the non-obvious resonance left by her heroine, herself now mostly forgotten, but vividly present in the structures she co-created, as well as in the principles of doing research which she taught.

References

Baba, Marietta L. (2009). W. Lloyd Warner and the anthropology of institutions: An approach to the study of work in late capitalism. *Anthropology of Work Review*, 30(2), 29–49.

Behar, Ruth (1993). *Translated Woman: Crossing the Border with Esperanza's Story*. Boston, MA: Beacon Press.

Berger, John (1991). *About Looking*. New York: Vintage International.

Beverungen, Armin, Steffen Böhm and Chris Land (2015). Free labour, social media, management: Challenging Marxist organization studies. *Organization Studies*, 36(4), 473–489.

Bieler Patrick, Milena D. Bister, Janine Hauer, Martina Klausner, Jörg Niewöhner, Christine Schmid and Sebastian von Peter (2021). Distributing reflexivity through co-laborative ethnography. *Journal of Contemporary Ethnography*, 50(1), 77–98.

Boje, David M. (1995). Stories of the storytelling organization: A postmodern analysis of Disney as 'Tamara-Land'. *Academy of Management Journal*, 38(4), 997–1035.

Burke, Kenneth (1945). *A Grammar of Motives*. Berkeley, CA: University of California Press.

Campbell, Joseph (1988). *The Inner Reaches of Outer Space: Metaphor as Myth and as Religion*. New York: Harper & Row.

Chia, Robert (1995). From modern to postmodern organizational analysis. *Organization Studies*, 16(4), 579–604.

Clifford, James and George Marcus (eds) (1986). *Writing Culture: The Poetics and Politics of Ethnography*. Berkeley, CA: University of California Press.

Cooper, Robert and Gibson Burrell (1988). Modernism, postmodernism and organizational analysis: An introduction. *Organization Studies*, 9(1), 91–112.

Cooren, François, Timothy Kuhn, Joep P. Cornelissen and Timothy Clark (2011). Communication, organizing and organization: An overview and introduction to the special issue. *Organization Studies*, 32(9), 1149–1170.

Counihan, Carole and Susanne Højlund (eds) (2018). *Making Taste Public: Ethnographies of Food and the Senses*. London, UK: Bloomsbury.

Czarniawska, Barbara (1999). *Writing Management: Organization Theory as a Literary Genre*. Oxford, UK: Oxford University Press.

Czarniawska, Barbara (2014). *Social Science Research: From Field to Desk*. London, UK: SAGE.

Czarniawska-Joerges, Barbara (2007). *Shadowing: And Other Techniques for Doing Fieldwork in Modern Societies*. Copenhagen, Denmark: Copenhagen Business School Press.

d'Aubuisson, Juan José Martínez (2019). *A Year Inside MS-13: See, Hear, and Shut Up*. New York: OR Books.

de Certeau, Michel (1988 [1974]). *The Practice of Everyday Life*. Berkeley, CA: University of California Press.

Deal, Terrence and Kennedy, Allan (2000 [1982]). *Corporate Cultures: The Rites and Rituals of Corporate Life*. New York: Basic Books.

Deleuze, Giles (1992). Postscript on the Societies of Control, *October*, 59, 3–7.

Denzin, Norman K. (1992). *Symbolic Interactionism and Cultural Studies: The Politics of Interpretation*. Hoboken, NJ: John Wiley & Sons.

Donati, Pierpaolo and Margaret Archer (2015). *The Relational Subject*. Cambridge, UK: Cambridge University Press.

Eco, Umberto (1989 [1962]). *The Open Work (Opera aperta: Forma e indeterminazione nelle poetiche contemporanee)*. Cambridge, MA: Harvard University Press.

Eco, Umberto (1990). *The Limits of Interpretation*. Bloomington, IN: Indiana University Press.

Elidrissi, Yousra Rahmouni and David Courpasson (2021). Body breakdowns as politics: Identity regulation in a high-commitment activist organization. *Organization Studies*, 42(1), 35–59.

Emerson, Robert M., Rachel I. Fretz and Linda L. Shaw (2011). *Writing Ethnographic Fieldnotes*. Chicago, IL: University of Chicago Press.

Evans-Pritchard, Edward Evan (1928). The dance. *Africa*, 1(4), 446–462.

Evans-Pritchard, Edward Evan (1976). *Witchcraft, Oracles and Magic among the Azande (Abridged Edition)*. Oxford, UK: Oxford University Press.

Fontana, Andrea and James H. Frey (1994). Interviewing: The art of science. In Norman K. Denzin and Yvonne S. Lincoln (eds), *Collecting and Interpreting Qualitative Materials*, London, UK: SAGE, 47–78.

Fornstedt, Helena (2021). *Innovation Resistance: Moving Beyond Dominant Framings*. Uppsala, Sweden: Uppsala Universitet.

Förster, Till (2022). Bodily ethnography: Some epistemological challenges of participation, *Ethnography*, online first February 4. https://doi.org/10.1177/14661381211067452.

Gabriel, Yiannis (2004). Introduction. In Y. Gabriel (ed.), *Myths, Stories and Organizations: Premodern Narratives for our Times*. Oxford, UK: Oxford University Press, 1–10.

Gadamer, Hans-Georg (2006 [1960]). *Truth and Method*, 2nd rev. ed. New York: Continuum.

Gaggiotti, Hugo, Monika Kostera and Paweł Krzyworzeka (2017). More than a method? Organisational ethnography as a way of imagining the social, *Culture and Organization*, 23(5): 325–340. https://doi.org/10.1080/14759551.2016.1203312

Geertz, Clifford (1973). *The Interpretation of Cultures*. New York: Basic Books.

Geertz, Clifford (2000). *Available Light: Anthropological Reflections on Philosophical Topics*. Princeton, NJ: Princeton University Press.

Gillespie, Richard (1993). *Manufacturing Knowledge: A History of the Hawthorne Experiments*. Cambridge, UK: Cambridge University Press.

Goffman, Erving (1959). *The Presentation of Self in Everyday Life*. New York: Doubleday.

Goodall, H.L. (Bud). (2000). *Writing the New Ethnography*. Lanham, MD: AltaMira Press.

Gudkova, Svetlana (2018). Interviewing in qualitative research. In Małgorzata Ciesielska and Dariusz Jemielniak (eds), *Qualitative Methodologies in Organization Studies*. London, UK: Palgrave Macmillan, 75–96.

Gupta, Akhil and James Ferguson (1997). Discipline and practice: 'The field' as site, method, and location in anthropology. In *Anthropological Locations: Boundaries and Grounds of a Field Science*. Berkeley, CA and London, UK: University of California Press, pp. 1–47.

Hammersley, Martyn and Paul Atkinson (2019). *Ethnography Principles in Practice.* London, UK: Routledge.

Harding, Nancy and Monika Kostera (2021). Doing ethnography: Introduction. In M. Kostera and N. Harding (eds), *Organizational Ethnography.* Cheltenham, UK; Northampton, MA: Edward Elgar Publishing, pp. 1–17.

Hastings, Catherine, Angela Davenport and Karen Sheppard (2022). The loneliness of a long-distance critical realist student: the story of a doctoral writing group. *Journal of Critical Realism*, 21(1), 65–82.

Helin, Jenny (2020). Temporality lost: A feminist invitation to vertical writing that shakes the ground. *Organization.* https://doi.org/10.1177/1350508420956322

Hochschild, Arlie Russel (1983). *The Managed Heart: Commercialization of Human Feeling.* Berkeley, CA: University of California Press.

Holmes, Douglas (2000). *Integral Europe: Fast-Capitalism, Multiculturalism, Neofascism.* Princeton, NJ: Princeton University Press.

Holstein, James A. and Jaber F. Gubrium (1997). Active interviewing. In: David Silverman (ed), *Qualitative Research: Theory, Method and Practice.* London, UK: Sage.

Höpfl, Heather (2002). Hitchcock's *Vertigo* and the tragic sublime. *Journal of Organizational Change Management*, 15(1), 21–34.

Höpfl, Heather and Stephen Linstead (1993). Passion and performance: Suffering and carrying the organizational roles. In S. Fineman (ed.), *Emotion in Organizations.* London, UK: SAGE, pp. 76–93.

Humphrey, Caroline (1983). *Karl Marx Collective: Economy, Society and Religion in a Siberian Collective Farm.* Cambridge, UK: Cambridge University Press.

Hylland Eriksen, Thomas (2015). *Fredrik Barth: An Intellectual Biography.* London, UK: Pluto.

Hymes, Dell (1996). *Ethnography, Linguistics, Narrative Inequality: Toward an Understanding of Voice.* Abingdon, UK: Routledge.

Jackson, Michael (2012). *Lifeworlds: Essays in Existential Anthropology.* Chicago, IL: University of Chicago Press.

Jaffe, Alexandra (1995). The limits of detachment: A non-ethnography of the military. *NAPA Bulletin*, 16(1), 36–47.

Jaquet, Chantal (2010). *Philosophie de l'odorat.* Paris, France: Presses Universitaires de France.

Jensen, Tommy and Johan Sandström (2019). *Organizing Rocks.* Accessed on 3 November 2021 at https://www.organizingrocks.org/

Jensen, Tommy and Johan Sandström (2021). *Gruvans makt.* Luleå, Sweden: Black Island Books.

Johansson, Ulla (1998). *Om ansvar: Ansvarsföreställningar och deras betydelse för den organisatoriska verkligheten.* Lund, Sweden: Lund University Press.

Jones, Delmos (1970). Towards a native anthropology. *Human Organization*, 29(4), 251–259.

Jung, Carl Gustav (1981 [1934]). *The Archetypes and the Collective Unconscious. Collected Works*, 9 (2 ed.), Princeton, NJ: Bollingen.

Kearney, Richard (2021). *Touch: Recovering our Most Vital Sense.* New York: Columbia University Press.

Kelley, Tom and Jonathan Littman (2005). *The Ten Faces of Innovation: IDEO's Strategies for Beating the Devil's Advocate and Driving Creativity throughout Your Organization.* New York: Doubleday.

Kenway, Jane and Aaron Koh (2013). The elite school as 'cognitive machine' and 'social paradise': Developing transnational capitals for the national 'field of power'. *Journal of Sociology*, 49(2–3), 272–290.

Kohn, Tamara and Cris Shore (2017). The ethics of university ethics committees: Risk management and the research imagination. In S. Wright and C. Shore (eds), *Death of the Public University? Uncertain Futures for Higher Education in the Knowledge Economy*. New York: Berghahn Books, pp. 229–249.

Kostera, Monika (2012). *Organizations and Archetypes*. Cheltenham, UK; Northampton, MA: Edward Elgar Publishing.

Kostera, Monika (2021). Observation: On the importance of being there. In Monika Kostera and Nancy Harding (eds), *Organizational Ethnography*. Cheltenham, UK; Northampton, MA: Edward Elgar Publishing, pp. 31–44.

Kostera, Monika and Anna Modzelewska (2021). To look at the world from the Other's point of view: Interview. In Monika Kostera and Nancy Harding (eds), *Organizational Ethnography*. Cheltenham, UK; Northampton, MA: Edward Elgar Publishing, pp. 74–90.

Krzyworzeka, Amanda (2013). Decision-making in farming households in eastern Poland. *Focaal. Journal of Global and Historical Anthropology*, 2013(65), 129–144.

Krzyworzeka, Paweł and Rodak Olga (2013). Jak (nie) przygotowywać studentów do pracy w biznesie. *Etnografia Polska*, 57(1–2), 105–117.

Kunat, Beata (2015). Pomiędzy sztuką a badaniem naukowym: Etnografia wizualna jako źródło wiedzy o rzeczywistości edukacyjnej. *Pogranicze: Studia Społeczne*, XXVI, 89–101.

Kunda, Gideon (1992). *Engineering Culture: Control and Commitment in a High-tech Corporation*. Philadelphia, PA: Temple University Press.

Lee, Raymond M. (1994). *Dangerous Fieldwork*. London, UK: SAGE Publications.

Letiche, Terrence (2021) *Résonance de l'art au travail*. Doctoral thesis. Paris, France: Université de Paris-Saclay.

Letiche, Hugo and Jean-Luc Moriceau (2019). Introduction: Pour art du sens pluriel. In Jean-Luc Moriceau, Hugo Letiche and Marie-Astrid Le Theule (eds), *L'art du sens dans les organizations*. Quebec, Canada: Les Presses de l'Universié Laval, pp. 1–26.

Lévi-Strauss, Claude (1975). Anthropology: Preliminary definition: Anthropology, ethnology, ethnography. *Diogenes*, 23(90), 1–25.

Lincoln, Yvonne S. and Egon G. Guba (1985). *Naturalistic Inquiry*. Beverly Hills, CA: SAGE.

Malinowski, Bronisław (1967). *A Diary in the Strict Sense of the Term*. London, UK: Routledge.

Mandalaki, Emmanouela and Mar Pérezts (2020). It takes two to tango: Theorizing inter-corporeality through nakedness and eros in researching and writing organizations. *Organization*, online first https://doi.org/10.1177/1350508420956321

Mangham, Iain L. and Michael A. Overington (1987). *Organizations as Theatre: A Social Psychology of Dramatic Appearances*. Chichester, UK; New York; Brisbane, Australia; Toronto, Canada; Singapore: John Wiley.

Marcus, George A. (1995). Ethnography in/of the world system: The emergence of multi-sited ethnography. *Annual Review of Anthropology*, 24(1), 95–117.

Marquand, John P. (1949). *Point of No Return*. Boston, MA: Little, Brown and Company.

Martin, Joanne (2002). *Organizational Culture: Mapping the Terrain*. Thousand Oaks, CA: SAGE Publications Inc.

Matošević, Andrea (2021). *Almost, but Not Quite Bored in Pula: An Anthropological Study of the Tapija Phenomenon in Northwest Croatia.* Oxford, UK: Berghahn Books.

Mnemosyne Atlas (2013–2016 [1927]). *Mnemosyne: Wanderings through Aby Warburg's Atlas.* The Warburg Institute, Cornell University Press, retrieved on 28 October 2021 at https://warburg.library.cornell.edu/about

Morauta, Louise, Ann Chowning, Current Issues Collective (B. Kaspou and Others), Angela M. Gilliam, Fritz Hafer, Diane Kayongo-Male, Hal B. Levine, Robert F. Maher, Khalil Nakleh, Jacob L. Simet, A.J. Strathern, C.A. Valentine, Bettylou Valentine and John Waiko (1979). Indigenous anthropology in Papua New Guinea [and comments and reply]. *Current Anthropology*, 20(3), 561–576.

Morgan, Gareth (1998). *Images of Organization.* Thousand Oaks, CA: SAGE.

Moriceau, Jean-Luc, Hugo Letiche and Marie-Astrid Le Theule (eds) (2019). *L'art du sens dans les organizations.* Quebec, Canada: Les Presses de l'Universié Laval.

Moss, Keith and Robert McMurray (2017). *Urban Portraits: Photography.* London, UK: Coffee Shop Photography.

Mumby, Dennis K. (2016). Organizing beyond organization: Branding, discourse, and communicative capitalism. *Organization*, 23(6), 1–24.

Narayan, Kirin (1993). How native is a 'native' anthropologist? *American Anthropologist*, 95(3), 671–686.

Nathan, Rebekah (2006). *My Freshman Year: What a Professor Learned by Becoming a Student, Reprint edition.* New York: Penguin Books.

Newton, Esther (1993). My best informant's dress: The erotic equation in fieldwork. *Cultural Anthropology*, 8(1), 3–23.

Ochinowski, Tomasz (2017). Przypominanie organizacyjne jako kompetencja. *Problemy Zarządzania*, 2(68), 39–53.

OECD (2020). *How's Life? 2020: Measuring Well-being.* OECD.

Pachirat, Timothy (2018). *Among Wolves: Ethnography and the Immersive Study of Power.* New York: Routledge.

Pink, Sarah (2009). *Doing Sensory Ethnography.* London, UK: SAGE.

Pink, Sarah (2021). *Doing Visual Ethnography.* London, UK: SAGE.

Polanyi, Michael (2009). *The Tacit Dimension.* Chicago, IL: University of Chicago Press.

Reddy, William M. (2001). *The Navigation of Feeling: A Framework for the History of Emotions.* Cambridge, UK: Cambridge University Press.

Riach, Kathlees and Samantha Warren (2015). Smell organization: Bodies and corporeal porosity in office work. *Human Relations*, 68(5), 789–809.

Rosa, Hartmut (2019). *Resonance: A Sociology of our Relationship to the World.* Cambridge, UK: Polity.

Sandberg, Sveinung (2008). Street capital: Ethnicity and violence on the streets of Oslo. *Theoretical Criminology*, 12(2), 153–171.

Schwartz-Shea, Peregrine and Dvora Yanow (2012). *Interpretive Research Design: Concepts and Processes.* New York: Routledge.

Shortt, Harriett and Samantha Warren (2017). Grounded visual pattern analysis: Photographs in organizational field studies. *Organizational Research Methods*, 22(1), 539–563.

Silverman, David (1993). *Interpreting Qualitative Data: Methods for Analysing Talk, Text, and Interaction.* London, UK: SAGE.

Simpson, Bob (2011). Ethical moments: Future directions for ethical review and ethnography. *Journal of the Royal Anthropological Institute*, 17, 377–393.

Sköldberg, Kaj (1990). *Administrationens poetiska logik: Stilar och stilförändringar i konsten att organisera*. Lund, Sweden: Studentlitteratur.

Sokolewicz, Zofia (2019). Cezaria Baudouin de Courtenay Ehrenkreutz-Jędrzejewiczowa – Uczona i organizatorka. In Ewa Bogacz-Wojtanowska i Monika Kostera (red.) *Siłaczki, szefowe społeczniczki: Polki, organizatorki*. Kraków, Poland: WUJ, s. 57–74.

Spoelstra, Sverre (2005). Robert Cooper: Beyond organization. *The Sociological Review*, 53(1), 106–119.

Stevenson, Lisa (2014). *Life Beside Itself: Imagining Care in the Canadian Arctic*. Oakland, CA: University of California Press.

Strati, Antonio (1999). *Organization and Aesthetics*. London, UK: SAGE.

Strati, Antonio (2021). Art and organizing: A brief personal reflection. In Monika Kostera and Cezary Woźniak (eds), *Aesthetics, Organization and Humanistic Management*. New York: Routledge, pp. 11–21.

Van Maanen, John (1988). *Tales of the Field: On Writing Ethnography*. Chicago, IL; London, UK: University of Chicago Press.

Van Maanen, John (1995). An end to innocence: The ethnography of ethnography. In J. Van Maanen (ed.), *Representation in Ethnography*. Thousand Oaks, CA; London, UK; New Delhi, India: SAGE, pp. 1–35.

Vindrola-Padros, Cecilia and Bruno Vindrola-Padros (2018). Quick and dirty? A systematic review of the use of rapid ethnographies in healthcare organisation and delivery. *BMJ Quality & Safety*, 24(4), 321–330.

Warren, Samantha (2012). Having an eye for it: Aesthetics, ethnography and the senses. *Journal of Organizational Ethnography*, 1(1), 107–118.

Wästerfors, David (2019). Den etnografiskt okänsliga etikgranskningen. *Statsvetenskaplig Tidskrift*, 121(2), 173–205.

Watson, Tony (2011). Ethnography, reality and truth: The vital need for studies of 'how things work' in organizations an management. *Journal of Management Studies*, 48(1), 202–217.

Weick, Karl E. (1995). *Sensemaking in Organizations*. Thousand Oaks, CA: SAGE.

Weiner, Annette B. (1976). *Women of Value, Men of Renown: New Perspectives in Trobriand Exchange*. Austin, TX: University of Texas Press.

Welsch, Wolfgang (1997). *Undoing Aesthetics*. London, UK: SAGE.

Wenders, Wim (1987). *Wings of Desire*. Argos Films.

Whyte, William Foote (1993). *Street Corner Society: The Social Structure of an Italian Slum*. Chicago, IL: University of Chicago Press.

Willis, Paul (1990). *Common Culture: Symbolic Work at Play in the Everyday Cultures of the Young*. Milton Keynes, UK: Open University Press.

Willis, Paul (2000). *The Ethnographic Imagination*. Cambridge, UK: Polity.

Winroth, Karin (1999). *När management kom till advokatbyrån: Om professioner, identitet och organisering*. Göteborg, Sweden: BAS.

Wright, Susan (1994). Culture in anthropology and organizational studies. In S. Wright (ed.), *Anthropology of Organizations*. London, UK; New York: Routledge, pp. 1–31.

Wulff, Helena (2020). *Ballet across Borders: Career and Culture in the World of Dancers*. London, UK: Routledge.

Yanow, Dvora (2009). Organizational ethnography and methodological angst: Myths and challenges in the field. *Qualitative Research in Organizations and Management: An International Journal*, 4(2), 186–199.

Yanow, Dvora (2018). Series editor's foreword. In T. Pachirat, *Among Wolves: Ethnography and the Immersive Study of Power*. New York: Routledge, pp. xi–xii.

Zagrzejewska, Ida (2008). *Wszechpolacy w galaktyce Gutenberga: o stosowaniu przemocy symbolicznej jako metodzie budowania relacji w organizacji, na przykładzie działalności Koła Młodzieży Wszechpolskiej w Białymstoku.* Undergraduate Thesis, Institute of Ethnology and cultural Anthropology, Warsaw University.
Zueva, Anna (2021). Autoethnography through the folk tale lens. In M. Kostera and N. Harding (eds), *Organizational Ethnography*. Cheltenham, UK; Northampton, MA: Edward Elgar Publishing, pp. 151–165.
Zyphur, Michael J., Dean C. Pierides and Jon Roffe (2016). Measurement and statistics in 'organization science': philosophical, sociological and historical perspectives. In R. Mir, H. Willmott and M. Greenwood (eds), *The Routledge Companion to Philosophy in Organization Studies*. London, UK: Routledge, pp. 474–482.

Index

Printed and bound by CPI Group (UK) Ltd, Croydon, CR0 4YY

13/04/2025

14656454-0002